THE

Get-Started

GUIDE TO

E-Commerce

THE

Get-Started

GUIDE TO

E-Commerce

Danielle Zilliox

AMACOM
American Management Association
New York • Atlanta • Boston • Chicago • Kansas City • San Francisco • Washington, D. C.
Brussels • Mexico City • Tokyo • Toronto

Special discounts on bulk quantities of AMACOM books are
available to corporations, professional associations, and other
organizations. For details, contact Special Sales Department,
AMACOM, a division of American Management Association,
1601 Broadway, New York, NY 10019.
Tel.: 212-903-8316. Fax: 212-903-8083.
Web site: www.amacombooks.org

This publication is designed to provide accurate and authoritative
information in regard to the subject matter covered. It is sold with
the understanding that the publisher is not engaged in rendering
legal, accounting, or other professional service. If legal advice or
other expert assistance is required, the services of a competent professional person should be sought.

Library of Congress Cataloging-in-Publication Data

Zilliox, Danielle.
    The get-started guide to e-commerce : getting online, creating successful Web
sites, order fulfillment, getting noticed / Danielle Zilliox.
        p.   cm.
    Includes index.
    ISBN 0-8144-7117-X
    1. Electronic commerce.   2. Web sites.   I. Title.
    HF5548.32.Z55   2001
    658.8'4—dc21 2001018176

This is a Leading Edge Press book.

Book design by Richard Oriolo

Printing number

10 9 8 7 6 5 4 3 2 1

To
Gail Williams,
for your unswerving support.

Contents

Chapter 4: Building the Page   57

Chapter 5: Behind the Scenes   116

Chapter 6: Making It Sell   141

THE

Get-Started

GUIDE TO

E-Commerce

Introduction

Back in the late 1960s, when computers were still the size of Buicks, the Department of Defense had a brilliant idea: Why not link several terminals in order to increase their power? The project was a great success, and during the next decade these newfangled networks experienced exponential growth—they rapidly became both more complex and more practical. Before long, scientists and academics across the country were getting involved in this onetime military program, awed by its incredible potential. They began sharing information with one another, linking their databases and communicating via electronic messages. The Internet was born.

Throughout the 1980s and early '90s, the Internet matured. Programmers developed today's standard formatting and hypertext protocols, and the computers themselves became smaller, faster, and cheaper. Versatility increased as new applications began to flood the market. By the time 1993 rolled around, the Internet was poised to explode into mainstream America—and it did.

Although the World Wide Web has only been a part of the public conscience for a few years, it has already become a mainstay of everyday life. Most of us now deal with computers or the Internet on a regular basis. Yet even as they are changing the world for the better, they have also created a fundamental shift in the pattern of our lives. The truth is that the blinding pace of progress has left gaps in our comfort level.

Technology is a playground for the few. Most people still don't know quite what to make of computers. We can use them, at least to some degree, but it seems only an "elect" handful of programmers can actually understand and manipulate their inner workings. When your PC breaks down, the best you can do is bang on the monitor a few times and try some harsh language. In the end, you're probably forced to bring it to an expert and trust that they'll know how to fix it. You feel utterly helpless, and that can make computers intimidating. Unless you hold a computer science degree from MIT, you're pretty much stuck on the outside looking in.

This is especially true of the business world. You word process, use e-mail, maybe work spreadsheets like a pro, but when it comes to actually creating an application yourself, you suddenly feel way out of your league. Perhaps you have a real desire to bring your company online—or just increase its current online presence—but aren't quite sure where to start. It can certainly be confusing. After all, most books on e-commerce are designed for "techies" or big-time business consultants; they appear to be written entirely in secret acronyms: HTML, UML, SET, SGML, RDD, VAN, WAP, EFTPOS, . . . the list goes on. For the technical novice, they're intimidating enough to make you reconsider online business. The dense, code-packed language just makes you feel stupid.

Yet nothing could be further from the truth. These weighty texts seem so complicated because they are aimed at a specialized audience—those individuals who are already experts in cyberspace. Forget them! Creating a strong Internet presence does *not* require the ability to define "object-oriented programming," nor does it demand a flawless command of HTML—the standard Web site code. That's what *programmers* are for! You're already busy enough. The last thing you need is another pile of thick manuals to wade through.

That's where we come in. This book is written in clear, direct English and avoids the abstractions and techno-jargon that makes other texts so completely unreadable. We focus specifically on material useful to *you*, the Internet layperson: What information should we include on our Web page? What are the best ways to market the site? Are we ready to fulfill online orders? Our advice—provided in concise, topical segments—is quick and accessible, so that you can painlessly help your company get an edge in the global market.

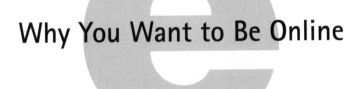

Chapter 1

Why You Want to Be Online

For the past few years, it has seemed that all anybody talks about is technology. Catchphrases like "information superhighway" and "Internet economy" are constantly bandied about, and a newly minted jargon is rapidly invading language across the globe: e-mail, e-tail, e-business —the list of e-words is pretty much endless. The barrage of cutting-edge technology surely heralds a revolution; and yet, this very transformation is not best evidenced by external changes in our tools or appliances. The real revolution is in the way we *think*. Indeed, the true impact of computers is felt within us—through our changing work habits and new ways to fill our leisure time, new perspectives and a faster pace of living. For better or worse, fewer people are finding it possible to enjoy quiet moments; we're working harder and for more hours than ever. For most of us, a clear-cut forty-hour week is simply out of the question!

Perhaps that is also what's so frightening about the whole experience. E-mail, the Internet, cell phones, and other such devices aren't just making the standard work easier; they're transforming the very nature of the work itself, and at a blinding pace. This powerful cyberwave has sent many people scrambling for a solid foothold, but the fact is that workplace stability is proving to be an elusive quality.

People respond to these forces in a typically human, mixed way. Some embrace the changes with unmitigated enthusiasm. You know the type: the CEO of the latest dot.com, the techno-geek, the young, fast-track business exec. Their excitement is palpable; aware of each "latest" advance almost before it happens, they are perpetually one step ahead of everybody else. With their comprehensive grasp of tech matters and a seemingly limitless ability to adapt, today's Internet leaders are both awe-inspiring and profoundly intimidating.

On the flip side of the coin, many individuals eschew the e-lifestyle at all costs. Comfortable with the tried-and-true ways of doing things, they are either uninterested in technology or afraid of the overwhelming changes it entails. Most of them don't yet own a personal computer, and even if their work necessitates one, they typically use it either for simple word processing or job-specific tasks. Of course there's nothing necessarily wrong with liking things the old-fashioned way; progress always does involve certain drawbacks. With so many devices keeping people tied to work on evenings and weekends, it's no wonder that many people prefer an "unplugged" peace of mind.

Unfortunately avoidance is no longer a viable option for the twenty-first-century businessperson. Computer literacy is increasing at a rapid pace. Almost 60 percent of U.S. households currently own a personal computer—and 20 percent of those who don't plan to buy one in the next year! In addition, the number of customers who use their PC to engage in e-commerce is skyrocketing: business-to-consumer (B2C) totals topped $33.1 billion in 1999, and continue to climb at the fantastic rate of about 85 percent each year. Such statistics present a powerful mandate to today's small business owners: adapt, or the world will pass you by.

By picking up this book, you're acknowledging the importance of integrating e-commerce into your life. Whether you're eager or reluctant, you realize that building a strong online presence is the key to business survival. This book will help you do that.

How the Internet Is Revolutionizing Business

No matter how scary computers can be, they're still changing the face of business—and mostly for the better. They're affecting the global economy in so many different ways that it's almost impossible to enumerate them all, much less predict what the average corporation will look like fifty years from now. Many science and computer magazines have published articles purporting to describe our "online future," but even the experts vary so greatly in their predictions that it's probably only safe to venture that our lives will be, well, *different*. Nevertheless, some things are quantifiable. Even if we can't predict the future, we can at least observe and discuss the current situation—and what an incredible situation it is!

> Almost any company can be global. Borders are becoming meaningless in the virtual world.

Instant Interaction

The improvements are due in large part to enhanced channels of communication. Web commerce is supremely "connective"—the Internet has the astounding ability to link over 400 million users worldwide, providing explosive, unprecedented growth in the potential market for every company on Earth. A home-manufacturer of fancy soaps can easily market her wares to customers from Wichita to Paris to Moscow if she so desires; she is no longer constrained by the physical limitations of print ads and word of mouth. The general irrelevance of geography has offered a huge boon to retailers working in niche markets. Specialty stores often experience difficulties growing because the clientele—though fiercely loyal—is limited in size. Say that Bob sells clown wigs in Salt Lake City. He makes the best wigs around, and every clown in Utah beats a path to his door, but after a certain point his clientele reaches a "critical mass" of sorts. There are only so many prospective Bozos in the area, so expansion becomes increasingly difficult as time passes. Bob might try to set up a side mail-order business, but he is still shackled by heavy advertising costs and delayed communication.

The Internet provides a shockingly simple answer. By obtaining the most basic Web site, Bob can market his hairpieces to anyone in the world with online access. Now he can compete for business from clowns in every U.S. state and scores of foreign countries as well; additionally, with a few inexpensive Web ads, Bob can watch his revenues increase exponentially. Now all he has to worry about is managing the logistics and raking in the profits! Modern technology has made commerce truly global.

Speed

Interaction is also faster than ever—whether from business to business (B2B) or business to consumer (B2C). E-mail is fast supplanting "snail mail" as the preferred mode of business communication; exchanges of the written word, even contracts, are no longer measured in days, but in hours or even minutes. Real-time chat offers companies the chance to immediately address the needs and concerns of both consumers and affiliates—even while both parties are online.

Toll-free numbers are rapidly becoming obsolete. The speed and efficiency are beneficial because they reduce transaction time, which is pleasing to both businesses and consumers.

Indeed, technology has transformed every industry with cheaper, universal communication at an unparalleled speed, yet that isn't too surprising. After all, the nature of progress has always been towards increased efficiency. Yet computers—paradoxically—also encapsulate traditionally small-business qualities by offering both unprecedented flexibility and personalization. In addition, they are doing much to democratize commerce, providing smaller companies a solid chance to compete with huge conglomerates. Big Business, the poster child of the industrial revolution, is now struggling to adapt as its power erodes. Bulk and bureaucracy have become liabilities. E-commerce favors companies that embrace change.

Adaptability

Flexible companies succeed because the Web is an entirely plastic medium, in that it can be stretched, molded, and remolded into any shape the user so desires. Although our lives are changing at a truly frenetic pace, the Internet responds by changing right with us. Newspapers offer us daily news, but online sites can update current events to the hour. For instance, if a manufacturer changes the price of one of its most popular products, it can merely repost the corrected information. Flyers, on the other hand, cannot be recalled and adjusted once they have been mailed out. E-mail and virtual chat also allow companies to receive and process instant feedback—and then immediately respond to the consumers' preferences. Mutual interaction requires companies to adapt, but it also enhances their ability to serve their clientele. On that note, we come to another important benefit of Internet technology: mass customization.

In the virtual world, it's now possible to both mass-produce *and* personalize your goods.

Mass Customization

Ever since Henry Ford popularized the assembly line, mass production has been the predominant retail philosophy. It certainly has its advantages; it allows businesses to churn out large quantities of product at a fairly low cost. This technique has been very successful for a long time, but it isn't without weaknesses. Mass production makes a standard product, no matter how many different colors or shapes are available, and customers are often forced to choose between settling for a product that doesn't quite suit them, or simply going without. Toys, computers, and jewelry are all examples of such large production-scale items. In some cases, personalization is possible—as with flower shops and tailors—but the added expense and delay often make such alternatives more undesirable than generic items.

Online business resolves this long-standing dilemma, enabling a seamless compromise between the two styles of production; the corporate world is calling it mass customization. In other words, businesses are able to produce each catalog item to the exact specifications of the consumer—*and* do so on a large scale. Interactive Web sites and online purchasing have made this possible; little girls can now design and name their own Barbie dolls online, have them delivered within a few days for a reasonable price, and all without even having to go near a car, much less spend all day shopping around. Customers are thrilled that their individual tastes have been directly addressed. In the same vein, companies can mass-customize the information they provide so that shoppers don't need to wade through information they don't want. The need to identify broad target audiences is no longer necessary. This technique enables Web programmers to build a site that adapts perfectly to each unique person who clicks through.

But customization does not merely benefit consumers. Businesses are pleased to be able to keep up large-scale production—they can personalize their products without having to shrink output to cottage-industry standards. In addition, making items to order helps companies maintain that all-important low inventory. The fewer items sitting idly in a warehouse, the better the profits are. Mass customization is a great way to support your efforts to achieve Just In Time (JIT) production!

Equality

Smaller companies greatly benefit from another characteristic of the virtual marketplace: democratization. Since the dawn of commerce, private start-up companies have had to fight tooth-and-nail to compete with large, established corporations. (When early man first opened his Stone Shoppe, he was probably soon crushed by Big Harry's Discount Rock Warehouse.) Sometimes building and maintaining a business niche can seem an insurmountable task. The big guys have deep pockets and brand-name recognition while small companies are saddled with large debts and near-anonymity. Being an entrepreneur is tough, and countless businesses have been choked out by the corporate machine. Now, at last, the tide is turning: the Internet is offering the little guys the chance to stand on more equal footing with big business. The ease and low pricing of Web advertising lets any company throw a substantial hat into the ring. When a browsing customer searches certain key words, he's going to pick whichever site seems the best, and in the virtual world, size really doesn't matter as much. If you take the time to build a quality Web site, your storefront can look truly professional. Granted, you'll still have to compete with famous brands, but at least now you have the resources to establish your *own* name. In addition, you actually have one solid advantage over large corporations—as a smaller company, you have flexibility. You may not be able to slay Goliath, but at least you can eat into his profits!

Who needs middlemen when you can do it quicker and cheaper yourself?

Simplification

As technology grows in complexity, it surprisingly is also beginning to shed its thick bureaucratic skin. Customarily, the intricacies of machines have created immense quantities of red tape around businesses. It's often hard to make a simple purchase request at many companies; the order is routed through so many people in so many different positions that the request can take days or even weeks. Middlemen—whether intermediate people or processes—have long been a fixture in large businesses. The Internet is changing all of that. The intermediaries are fading into the background, hence the term "disintermediation."

The speed and immediacy of the Web has enabled countless business to begin the long process of eliminating redundant people and practices. If your name is A, and you have a message for B, why should you have to first send it through C and D? It sounds ridiculous, but many employees have been forced to do this for years. Now the trend is reversing.

The same is true of relations between separate companies. Products usually travel a long, circuitous route before they arrive on store shelves. The raw materials are manufactured by certain companies, which then send the components to a different business to be assembled into a finished product. The products are often then transported to distributors, which monitor demand and make the necessary shipments to retailers. Actual bricks-and-mortar stores only come into play at the end of the road.

New technology has helped streamline this lengthy process—if a manufacturer can use the Internet to track product sales and demand, then it can begin making shipments directly to the stores itself. In addition, the option of building an online store makes it viable for the manufacturer to even sell directly to the customers! This is revolutionary; in the real world, no shopper would visit and make purchases from a crowded, noisy factory floor. For one thing, consumers prefer the cleanliness and organization of an ordinary storefront. In addition, manufacturers must adhere to a limited product line: they can only sell what they personally make. These restrictions used to make it more attractive for customers to shop at traditional stores, which can stock a few items from hundreds or even thousands of different manufacturers. Who wants to drive to four different places just to complete the errands?

Yet now, factory Web sites can exhibit every convenience and amenity of a normal online store. Most customers probably wouldn't be able to tell the difference between an online manufacturer and an online e-tailer, if both sell the same product. Merchandise variety is also less of a factor. Internet stores, no matter what their Web address, are located only a few keystrokes away from every other store. It's no longer so inconvenient to shop at six different stores in one afternoon—and it can be markedly less expensive. That's the beauty of wholesale: low prices. But affordability is not just a customer benefit; it applies to businesses as well.

Affordability

E-technology has certainly revolutionized commerce. It has cleared the path to new methods of marketing and communicating, elevating business sophistication to unprecedented levels. Yet despite the increased complexity, successful Web ventures can be surprisingly cheap! The price of a basic Web site, used only for shopping, is limited to the negligible price of a URL and a few staff hours per week. If you throw in some advertising, the additional cost is easily offset by the increase in business.

Building an online purchasing site, where customers can buy your product online, does of course require a great deal of planning and expense. Yet once again, if you're careful, the benefits of strengthening your Internet presence will outweigh the costs. The incredible economy of the Web is one of the main reasons that smaller companies can compete with corporations. E-mail is virtually free; advertising is relatively inexpensive; upkeep of a large site is markedly cheaper than upkeep of a large bricks-and-mortar store. The truth is, almost anyone can afford to venture online, and right now—if you play your cards carefully—almost anyone can find Internet success.

Although some risk is involved, it may be more dangerous for your company if you *don't* move online!

Believe it or not, smaller companies are the future of virtual business. They are making the transition to the Web in growing numbers, and it's not too late for you to join the movement! Even though your real-life, bricks-and-mortar company may be successful on its own, it's wise for the savvy manager to keep his or her business up-to-date. Online commerce in 1999 actually increased *120* percent over the previous year's totals. This is phenomenal growth! Those businesses that hesitate now are opting out on a potential gold mine. Consumers will be spending more and more of their money online, and those companies who fail to adapt will suffer the fiscal consequences. It's frightening, but it's the truth.

In addition, the emerging medium still leaves a surprising amount of room for *continued* growth. Online B2C commerce currently comprises only one or two percent of the entire economy. These two qualities—profitability and youth—illustrate both the popularity and potential of the Web. E-commerce is booming, but the relatively small market share indicates that it is not likely to plateau any time soon.

Yet ironically, as the Web market becomes saturated with myriad companies, it will become increasingly difficult to share the incredible fortune. Although consumers will be spending more money, the initial ventures will become more established. Customers will already have favorite Web sites, and the increasing brand-loyalty will make it more difficult for newcomers to establish a solid footing in cyberspace. Soon it will be too late to be a pioneer; search engines will drag up countless businesses similar to yours. Don't be just another e-tailer on an endless list. If you want to make a name for your company, you have to strike while the proverbial iron is hot.

Bricks-and-Mortar Companies

Of course, there is a certain amount of risk involved in building a Web site. Many readers doubtless recall the recent bad press regarding e-commerce—the reports that online business is all hype and no profit. That is indeed true of many Internet start-ups; they set their prices too low or falter at shipping logistics, and they eventually go belly-up. Sometimes the business concept itself simply isn't workable. Even huge industry names like Amazon.com have had serious difficulties. Believe it or not, the hugely popular book e-tailer is still operating in the red. Indeed, despite its undeniably large clientele, in over five years of business Amazon has yet to post a profitable quarter!

Out of necessity, such companies are relying on ever more cautious investors to shore up the financial gaps—which is why the tech stocks took a pretty heavy hit in 2000. Although nothing catastrophic is on the horizon, it's prudent for the growing business to be aware that in many ways, the Internet is like a war zone. Although everyone has a chance, not everyone wins. Cyberspace is littered with the corpses of failed ventures. In order to succeed, you must tread carefully and learn from both the victories *and* mistakes of others. Blindly rushing in often leads only to disappointment.

Bricks-and-mortar companies actually have the
Internet advantage!

Happily, there is good news. The companies that struggle the most online are usually Internet start-ups, or companies that exist only on the Web. Established bricks-and-mortar companies are a lot more likely to succeed. In fact, many analysts are currently predicting that in the scuffle amongst catalog retailers, dot.coms, and bricks-and-mortar companies, the traditional merchants will emerge as kings of the Internet. Even though large numbers of start-ups are struggling to stay afloat, fully 83 percent of bricks-and-mortar companies reported an increase in sales after moving online—and that's not even accounting for Web site quality!

Real-life companies are profitable for a variety of reasons. In the first place, they already have a solid clientele that knows the company pretty well. It's a ready-made revenue source. Consider your own business: It would be relatively easy to promote the site; you are already in contact with a number of people who will probably be interested. When compared with strangers who merely see your company name on a list of search results, your real-life customers are far more likely to visit your site, and they are also more likely to purchase something once there. After all, they're already familiar with your reliability and the quality of your product, and thus feel more comfortable turning their shopping trip into a buying one. Your preexisting reputation can thus be a real advantage for your Internet venture.

In addition, successful bricks-and-mortar companies already have all the pricing and logistics kinks worked out. The complex maze of data management necessary to any enterprise is largely complete: they already know approximately at what price they can afford to sell each item, they have solid relationships with the manufacturers, they've studied the target market segment—in other words, they're already experts in their own particular field. E-companies have to start with a few ideas and hope they pan out; bricks-and-mortar businesses have endured the testing stage and survived. Branching out from a solid core business is far easier than creating a brand new company.

Foster the Right Attitude

Before you make the commitment to move online, however, it is important for you to understand the two greatest mistakes that bricks-and-mortar managers make when moving online.

1. *This Web site will be an interesting experiment.* Traditional managers can be understandably tentative when developing and implementing a Web site for their company. Perhaps they don't feel personally comfortable with the technology, or maybe they're not sure if moving online is even a good idea. They thus decide to "try it out" before they do anything drastic. Bad idea. Because these leaders do not know exactly how far they want to go with the project, they fail to commit sufficient resources to create a good online storefront. They also shy away from developing an assertive business plan, which can cause serious problems (see Chapter 3). Such ambivalence is incredibly harmful. A site that is hastily constructed during somebody's lunch breaks will usually contain serious design flaws—and it will be obvious to customers that you do not take the online store seriously. And, if your Web site makes a poor initial showing, disappointed shoppers won't return. This can cause permanent damage.

2. *We must protect our core business.* A large percentage of bricks-and-mortar business managers are incredibly protective of their real-life operations. Although they may pay lip service to the Web site, they actually believe that it is only going to "steal"

profits from the main store. To some degree, this is a valid concern. Because of brutally competitive online prices, most virtual businesses have a smaller per-transaction profit than do bricks-and-mortar stores. Shackled by their deep-seated distrust, such managers fail to provide the enthusiasm and energy necessary to creating a quality venture. They are afraid to make the site truly competitive, because they don't want it to strangle the bricks-and-mortar business. Just as with the "experiment" approach, this attitude will cause the venture to drown in half-measures and lukewarm support. This is a huge mistake.

Before you move online, you must accept that, to a certain degree, you *will* be siphoning current customers away from the real world store. In other words: be willing to cannibalize your business. Granted, this runs contrary to instinct, and it might even harm profits in the near future, but it will almost certainly pay off in the long run. If you commit to a strong online operation, its success will eventually more than compensate for the losses you experience in the bricks-and-mortar store. Remember that the future of business is going to be played out on the Internet. If you hamstring your own virtual store, you'll only succeed in postponing the inevitable. Eventually, you will begin to lose traditional customers as more people shop online. If by then you have not already established a solid presence, your business will suffer.

These two attitudes are basically acts of self-sabotage. When you move online, you need to be aggressive and decisive—and perhaps even a little bit ruthless. If you are not comfortable enough with the idea to make a definite commitment, it is better to postpone the site until you can. E-commerce is a cutthroat field. It is not for the faint of heart. Once you go public, you'll be instantly affecting the way potential customers perceive your company. You must make sure that when you *do* open your doors for virtual business, you're ready for the consequences.

The purpose of this advice is not to frighten you away; on the contrary, the point of this whole book is to encourage small businesses to get involved in e-commerce. But you also need to know the facts. E-commerce is not a panacea for all your corporate ills. It would be foolish to assume success is guaranteed; more than one company has ended up *losing* business after moving online.

Yet, that doesn't have to be you. You can avoid this fate by making a solid, realistic commitment, studying your own personal situation and learning from those who went before you. More than one Web site has succumbed to follies like a bad design and poor follow-through, but such outcomes are hardly preordained. With the proper research, a lot of hard work, courage, and creativity, you can ensure that your venture meets with success.

Chapter 2

Analyzing Your Internet Potential

Online ventures are frequently lost before they're even off the starting blocks. The Internet rush can be so intoxicating that companies move onto the Web before they've really considered the nuts and bolts of the transition. They just hire an IT person or two (that's Information Technology) and ask them to design a Web site. Therein lies a critical error. IT people are an extremely intelligent and capable group on the whole, but their talents are in the details. They can construct Web pages and solve technical problems, yet they lack the thorough understanding of *your* company that only a manager can possess. Should you have online purchasing, or not? How about graphics? Should you link the site to your inventory? These are questions that must be assessed by business leaders prior to actual site construction, not decided on the fly by a new-hire.

....

Progress necessitates a strong sense of direction.

....

You need a big picture, as a full-bodied concept, in order to begin a journey. No sane person would attempt to drive from Seattle to Baton Rouge without a detailed map, and yet scores of companies are willing to pursue the goal of Web success without deciding exactly how to get there. You, as the manager of a growing business, need to provide a complete, informed "road map" even though you don't need to know HTML or XML backwards and forwards. You've got to be Web savvy.

Tailor Your Web Site to Your Product

The first step you need to take is deciding to what extent you believe your company should be online. Yes, financial considerations are important, as is the allocation of such physical resources as worker time and inventory, but you can't successfully weigh these issues without knowing what kind of site you can best support. And to do that, you need to take a long, hard look at your products and services.

The truth is that some business is simply hard to conduct in cyberspace. After all, you can't offer shoe-shines online, nor can you give haircuts or fix cars—technology just hasn't progressed that far! That does *not* mean that you can't or shouldn't support a Web site, but it does significantly affect the manifest purpose and thus design of your venture. Therefore, the nature of the company is a determining factor.

If you are a retailer, you're actually in pretty good shape. E-commerce is very friendly to tangible goods since they are easily represented (via pictures or specifications) and can usually be shipped without too much difficulty. If you fall into this category, it might be a good idea to provide for online purchasing, a service in which interested parties can actually buy your product at the site.

This is the most convenient avenue for the consumer, and convenience is paramount in e-commerce.

Customer satisfaction is obviously an overriding concern for all successful business managers, and customers as a group will *not* be satisfied if the site isn't highly efficient, regardless of your bargains or your cool site design. A whopping 79 percent of consumers report that convenience is the main reason why they shop online, despite the current hooplah over super-low prices. (That category scored barely half the percentage points raked in by convenience.) Of course, home delivery isn't always an option. If you sell tractors or something equally unwieldy, you might have to make other arrangements. Internet shoppers are still rather tentative about buying products online, but as they grow increasingly comfortable with the process, there will be an increasing demand for online purchasing options.

Even service-oriented business can—and *should*—develop an
online store!

Services are a different story. In the first place, unlike tangible goods, they're difficult to represent graphically. In some cases, such as haircuts or house-painting, you can post before-after photos. That helps, although it's not as convincing as the pictures of an actual product. But if you run a transportation service for the elderly, how do you represent a car ride? You can show the picture of a car or a smiling old lady, but that neither proves the true quality of the service nor helps answer the questions a customer may have.

Therefore, when it comes to marketing a service, you have to rely on words—descriptions of your company and reputation, explanations of your service, and customer testimonials as to quality. A picture may be worth a thousand words, but when pictures are inadequate, language will have to do. You also might have to do without online purchasing; most customers are still skittish about buying a product sight unseen.

All things considered, no matter what your business, you must be as concrete as possible about what you have to offer, whether that entails pictures, specifications, or explanations. Vague Web sites are almost always failures. All of these matters will be discussed in depth in Chapter 4.

Location, Location, Location

It's certainly exciting to be able to market your business worldwide with a simple Web page; indeed, global advertising can be advantageous to your company. But the relative low cost of a basic Web site can suddenly become your worst nightmare if you don't carefully consider the financial consequences of geography. Our present technology may be fairly advanced, but teleportation is still a long way off. If a guy in Taiwan orders a shirt, you're going to have to allow for the shipping costs to send that shirt halfway around the world. Of course, you could just charge the price to the customer, but the post office or UPS can easily run up tabs that exceed the actual price of the product itself. Who would buy a fifteen-dollar shirt that costs thirty to forty dollars with shipping? Most customers will just look somewhere closer to home. Then again, if you eat the cost, you'll lose money on the sale.

Don't overextend yourself—set limits.

It's often a better idea for many companies to limit their sales to a strictly defined geographical area. That way, they can better control shipping costs and maintain bargain prices. You should consult a shipping company to determine exactly how large a geographical area you can afford to service.

For people who sell services, it's usually even more important to limit sales. You certainly wouldn't be able to fly to Siberia just to lay down carpet for an interested customer. Yes, this example is extreme, but it illustrates an important point: Don't market your company to regions that you can't profitably support. Often, this simply means taking the limits you most likely already have in place and transferring them online. Decide in advance exactly which cities or zip codes are within range and which ones should be excluded. Then you can structure your site to cater especially to your chosen zone.

Analyze Your Human Resources

So-called "smaller companies" do not occupy as uniform a niche as the name might imply; they fulfill countless functions and employ anywhere from one to several hundred people. Before you even consider moving to the Web, you need to spend some quality time studying the structure of your company. Is your business equipped to handle a new branch of sales? You will need to allocate a certain number of employee hours to the maintenance and support of the site; exactly how much time depends upon the sophistication of the site and the existing size of your clientele. You may need to train customer support representatives to work mainly with the online customers; the accounting department needs to be ready to handle a new stream of costs as well as revenues; marketing must be able to take full advantage of Internet ad resources.

Indeed, building and operating a Web site is a full-time undertaking—if you are an entrepreneur and still the sole employee of your company, you'll almost certainly need to bring someone else on board to help out. The Internet requires a team effort, and those businesses that recognize the need for collaboration are far more likely to succeed in their endeavor. Once you have analyzed the probable impact of e-commerce on your employees, help ready them for the transition. Just don't forget to reinforce your policies on a day-to-day basis.

Talk to Your Customers

Never make the transition until you've consulted the most vital people of all: your customers. Understanding your own capabilities and resources is naturally important, but all of that means nothing if you lack the support of the people who actually buy from you. If you plunge in without discovering your patrons' needs, you're working blind, and thus risk sinking considerable expenditures into a doomed venture. Talk to the customers. Ask them to fill out surveys. To ensure a good rate of feedback, you can offer small incentives for each completed form: coupons, samples, whatever your company can best provide. Create a simple questionnaire that asks such questions:

1. Do you own a personal computer?
2. Do you have access to the Internet?
3. Do you use e-mail regularly?
4. Have you ever purchased anything online? If not, would you consider it in the near future?

Use the answers to help you decide what type of Web site to construct. If your customers are positively inclined toward and/or experienced with e-commerce, you probably want to invest in a complex site that can offer a variety of services. If you support a more traditional clientele, it might be a waste of time and money to build a fancy page complete with all the bells and whistles. Still, regardless of your customers' preferences, it's a good idea to post a basic "business card" information Web page. The experience will put you one step ahead as your customers become more comfortable in cyberspace. Besides, you might be able to attract a few new customers just by explaining your products or services and providing an 800 number.

Once you've analyzed the data, act on it—but remember to keep the communication lines open. A hesitant client base may become enthusiastic over the next few years; survey them at least once every six months, and monitor any changes. Remember that adaptability is the key to Internet survival.

Online Shopping vs. Online Purchasing

Once you've thoroughly considered all the above factors—finance, geography, human resources, and customer needs—you're ready to make the most important design decision about your Web page: Should it include online purchasing or not? Before you answer that question, it's a good idea to examine what each method entails. So what exactly *is* the difference between online shopping and online purchasing?

Online Shopping

Online shopping is a series of screens that describe your catalog of products while also establishing your company's reliability; it encompasses all the information consumers desire to have before making a purchase. But just how important is it?

Offline, before customers buy a product, they usually stop and look over the item first. If they have questions, they may ask a nearby salesperson. They need to amass a certain amount of data before they can feel comfortable purchasing it. Very rarely are shoppers willing to buy merchandise hastily and sight unseen, especially if it is somewhat expensive.

Online shopping provides the information and reassurance that most customers need to make informed decisions.

But aside from the product, customers also need to know something about the company. We rarely consider this need, but it does exist.

We just don't notice it because most bricks-and-mortar stores we shop at are well-established—or at least tangible. We can physically check the store over before making the decision to shop there.

Yet online, obtaining such information is much more difficult. The products themselves cannot be touched or handled; they can only be represented two-dimensionally. In addition, it can be hard to tell the difference between a legitimate company and a fraudulent one. In real life, companies are usually forced by the very permanence of the building to run a legal operation; on the Internet, it is much easier to establish a scam company and then abscond with the money into cyberspace oblivion.

It's no wonder, then, that almost all customers desire thorough online shopping information: It provides for both of these customer needs. Not only does this service help ensure quality goods, it helps guarantee that the company is legit! Because these qualities are important in virtually all transactions, you almost certainly need to have a shopping site if you're going online.

Online Purchasing

Online purchasing is another story. Even though the words "shopping" and "buying" are often used in the same context, they actually encompass two very different processes. Recall that shopping is the act of researching various products, weighing the possibilities, and making a choice. To put it more clearly, it's the "looking around" part of the process. You don't necessarily spend any money; you're merely preparing yourself to do so.

Buying—or purchasing—on the other hand, involves the actual exchange of money for goods or services. Shopping is prep work, purchasing is the follow-through. Online shopping is relatively simple because it's largely a one-way flow of information—from business to consumer. You merely need to post it in a clear and effective manner and be willing to field a few questions. Yet once a shopper decides to buy something, the necessary complexity of a site increases dramatically. It's fairly easy to create pages describing your specialty toys, and designate maybe one customer service representative to answer inquiries. Yet when one of those customers decides to buy online, suddenly there's a mountain of logistics to resolve, and numerous people involved in that one single sale. You need to coordinate manufacturers, distributors, accountants, and shipping people on top of the one service guy. For these reasons, it's a good idea to hold off on an online purchasing site until you have three things:

1. *A solid number of customers who are willing to buy your product online.* Use your survey data to help you decide how enthusiastic your clientele is about e-commerce.

2. *A thorough understanding of the potential impact of the site on your company.* You *must* have a solid grasp of the ways in which online purchasing will affect the current business structure; this includes the willingness to hire additional tech personnel and restructure other departments, as necessary.

3. *Experience with the mail- or phone-order process.* If your company produces a traditional mail-order catalog and/or takes phone orders, you're a lot more likely to experience a smooth transition to online purchasing. Do not combine your first e-commerce venture with your first attempts to succeed at online order fulfillment.

It's better to proceed slowly and get it right than to rush in unprepared. A hastily built purchasing site can cause serious customer service problems, from lengthy shipping delays to botched orders. If a new customer has an unsatisfactory first experience with your company, he is not likely to return; you may even lose some of your current clientele. So do your homework before you act.

Because this research can be so very time-consuming, you might want to post only a shopping site for a while. It would help you get your feet wet in cyberspace and make small improvements in your approach before you advance to the next stage. For practice, post an 800 order number on your shopping site. You can gain valuable fulfillment experience while studying your clientele's buying patterns and increasing your profits. The future online purchasing site will benefit from this experience.

In sum, online purchasing is unquestionably a complicated process. So—if its existence poses such thorny problems, why even bother with online purchasing? The main benefit of online purchasing is, of course, convenience. This single factor speaks volumes. Remember that an overwhelming majority of customers view convenience as the single most important quality to the experience! In addition, whether we like it or not, e-commerce is the future of business. The sooner you adapt to the new methods, the better your company will perform in coming years.

All things considered, make sure you consider carefully which option is best for *your* company before you make any decisions.

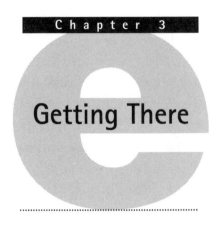

Chapter 3

Getting There

Now that you've studied the playing field, it's time to start putting your plans into action. Still, there's a ton of tasks to accomplish before you should start building that first Web page. Take your time. You need to lay the proper groundwork for the venture.

The Name Game

If you're not already online, the first thing you need to do is select your Web address—after all, before you build anything, you need a construction site. This is actually a very important stage. Your URL (short for the memorable phrase "uniform resource locator") is not just a random identifier like a telephone number; it's the word or phrase that many customers will need to memorize in order to reach the site. Sure, search engines can be helpful, but they'll also round up a ton of your competitors—with your business potentially buried at the bottom of a long list. So . . . you want customers to remember your address without resorting to a search command.

> Choose carefully. Your domain name should *not* be an afterthought!

Pretend that you sell action figures, and you want to advertise the new shopping site to your existing clientele. Telling them to visit www.actionfigures.com is a lot more likely to yield hits than www.action3462.com. It's also going to help you snare new business from customers who just happened to stumble on your name. (Nobody would ever "stumble" onto that second address!) Of course, nothing is ever this simple; companies are required to register their domain name, and no repeats are allowed. And, ever since the dot.com explosion, the bank of available names has been diminishing. So what to do when your first, second, and third choices are taken? It's time to get creative. Head over to www.icann.net, which keeps track of domain registration, and be willing to play around.

First try variations of the same name—maybe action-figures.com, action_figures.com, actionfigurez.com, or actionfigure.com. If that effort fails, be more specific; maybe joesactionfigures.com or coolactionfigures.com is still on the block. Companies that have a clearly predominant, best-selling item can often name the site after their breadwinner: captaindestruction.com might be available, especially if the product name is already patented. Still stuck? Go to www.networksolutions.com and use the MyNameFinder option. It'll let you input a couple key words and then spit out any combinations that are still unclaimed. Choose from among these, then go to a Web registrar and claim it. Just keep in mind that the address plus extension (.com, .org., .net, etc.) must be fewer than twenty-six characters.

Once you have an address, don't stop there. Protect your site by registering any unclaimed name similar to yours—make sure you at least try to reserve the different extensions or similar spellings. In essence, now that you've staked out territory, you must prevent other companies from riding your own profitable coattails by registering near-identical domain names. The slight additional expense of buying up extra names will be more than paid for since competitors will be unable to siphon off customers who type in near-miss URLs. Still, don't forget to pay your renewal bill on time. Losing your claim is a very unpleasant experience.

If you pay for domain names that you are not going to develop— at least yet—be prepared to explain and defend your actions. Internet authorities have recently been cracking down on those unethical individuals who make money by "cybersquatting," or by scalping popular domain names that they bought in expectation of a future profit. Such people buy any unregistered URL addresses that resemble the names and companies of famous people and institutions. They're betting that these parties will eventually look to build a Web site with those particular domains, and have to pay the involved cybersquatter for the privilege. For instance: If Joe Shmoe is the namesake of a huge conglomerate, Shmoe Corp., a squatter might register the domain names shmoecorp, shmoecorporation, and joeshmoe. This person doesn't actually intend to build a site to go with any of the addresses; he buys them up purely for the purpose of selling them to Joe later at a highly inflated price. In the meantime, the involved addresses are claimed but unused, which prompts the comparison with "squatting," a term that refers to people living illegally on someone else's land.

Currently, it is agreed that a purchase in expectation of further development is perfectly legal; it is the plan to sell the name for a profit that makes cybersquatting, like ticket scalping, an indefensible activity. If you can prove that you have a vested interest in the domain name, you will be allowed to hold it without immediately initiating any development. Authorities just want to make sure that people who register Internet names do so for a legitimate reason. As the matter now stands, you will only be brought up on charges if the victim lodges an official complaint. In the above example, it would have to be Joe or someone working for him in an official capacity. Even then, the punishment is usually just confiscation of the very intellectual property that led to the hearing. Nobody goes to jail for cybersquatting, but it's still an accusation that you want to avoid.

The Tax Tangle

You know the rule: Ignorance is not an acceptable excuse for breaking the law!

Before you do anything else, you need to seek legal counsel. The rules and regulations pertaining to e-commerce are not only different from those of bricks-and-mortar companies, but they change almost every day. They vary from county to county and from state to state. Don't worry about understanding them all; that's what tax attorneys are for. For the present, e-commerce is relatively unfettered by red tape, which is definitely good for you; but you still need to know how the law will affect your online venture *before* you go online. Perhaps you have a non-compete clause in the contract with your distributors. This would mean that you are not allowed to sell products directly to customers, because this would constitute competition with your current distribution partners. Obviously, that can have a profound impact on your venture—as can the other million regulations and contract clauses. So consult the experts. It'll save you a lot of trouble down the road.

Get Expert Help

Smaller companies can often get a bit caught up in all the excitement over the famed ease and accessibility of the World Wide Web. To some extent, the enthusiasm is warranted. The Internet does make it possible for ordinary business people to use high-tech, cutting edge technology. But that isn't always wise. Despite the glut of self-help programming texts on the market, you should probably avoid trying to construct your Web site on your own. After all, you're an amateur. So your Web site would probably wind up looking, well, amateurish.

Don't play around. Your Internet store is not a toy! Take the venture seriously—and hire serious help.

No matter what kind of site you build, even if it's one page of simple text, you want to hire at least one temporary IT (Information Technology) person. There's no reason for you to spend precious time learning HTML (a computer code used to build Web pages) when an expert can do a better job in a shorter amount of time. The best managers know how to delegate; you want to be deeply involved in the concept and design, but make sure you don't become mired in the details. Web designers can be paid by the hour—if you are willing to spend a couple hundred dollars, you can have a simple but professional-looking shopping site running in one afternoon. The money you spend on the designer is still cheaper than having to buy lots of dense programming books and wasting several days on the trial-and-error method. "Do-it-yourself" is not always the best option.

Nevertheless, you should still know some general information about the main programming languages in order to make intelligent hiring decisions. It's difficult to make any choices if you're not sure which questions to ask. When examining the credentials of a potential IT employee, or even if you're just evaluating your current staff, be sure to check their experience in the following languages.

- **HTML.** This is the big one. Anyone you hire to design and or build your store needs to be fluent in HyperText Markup Language; it's the basic building block of Web sites. HTML is actually not a true programming language. Indeed, it mostly determines the layout of a text document when it is transferred online. It consists largely of text interspersed with code "tags," or formatting directions for the document. The tags determine the placement and appearance of all regular text on each page.

  HTML files are usually like brochures; they might include pictures and interesting colors, but they are still essentially real-world documents that have been adjusted for online use. They are not true programs. Consider the following example:

  <HEAD><TITLE>Mike's Hawaiian Shirts</TITLE></HEAD>

  This line of code merely indicates that the given store name is the title of the document, and that it should be placed at the top of the page. So HTML is hardly cryptic or obscure; most lay-people can understand the basic principles with little difficulty. Actually, the language is almost *too* easy—many people have been lulled by its accessibility into trying to construct their virtual store on their own. Don't fall into this trap. It takes a great deal of practice to become truly fluent in the language, so you'll want your programmer to have considerable experience with writing HTML Web documents.

- **Java.** Unlike HTML, Java is a true, object-oriented programming language. It's a lot like C and C+ (popular non-Internet languages), but it's more universal; using Java, you can run the same application from virtually any type of computer. It thus more efficiently allows programmers to create applications for online use. In addition, whereas HTML serves an essentially aesthetic function, Java is normally employed to create objects that execute action and/or interaction. Popular Java applications include interactive forms, animation, clocks, search capabilities, hit counters, and more—all of which are incredibly useful to your store. Even though HTML code can be made to provide most of these functions, Java is by far the preferred method. Not surprisingly, because Java has more sophisticated capabilities, it's also a lot more difficult to learn than HTML; far fewer people are actually proficient in the language.

In response, Java developer Sun Microsystems has tried to make it more accessible, by making "pre-packaged" applications available to the general public. These objects are known as Java applets, and they have become quite popular with the programming community. Applets are self-contained bits of code that can independently perform various functions—they can also be imported into an HTML document, just like regular graphics. Thus, programmers can reap the benefits of the more powerful language without needing to be experts. It is now possible for relatively inexperienced programmers to create standard HTML Web pages with Java-enhanced functions—perhaps password protection and animated signs. Nevertheless, some knowledge of Java *is* required to make use of applets, and the best quality Web sites are still created by experts who can custom-fit the programs. If you can possibly afford it, you should find someone who has a solid grasp of the language. Remember: Your online store is not the proper place for experimentation.

• **XML.** No current e-commerce book is complete without a discussion of XML, or eXtensible Markup Language. Although HTML has long been the reigning bastion of online code, its days are numbered. Rapid progress in the field of computer programming has produced a better alternative to the old standard. XML, which blasted onto the scene in 1996, is now rapidly replacing HTML in the hearts of techies everywhere.

XML is the future of Internet programming. Hire someone who knows it.

One of the biggest problems in programming is system compatibility. It's unbelievably difficult to integrate computer systems when they are based on different languages, and it's costly as well. Linking incompatible systems is like trying to merge companies that cannot communicate with one another—it requires the development of a complex, custom translation interface to breach the gap. Thus, programmers work constantly to develop systems that can work either with older versions or with different languages altogether. XML is one successful result of such efforts. It can read and handle a number of other computer languages, including HTML.

It also has the revolutionary ability to use tags that describe the *content* of the data, rather than just its appearance. Instead of only being able to designate the location and size of a certain bit of text, the text can be placed according to its actual substance. In the product catalog for Mike's Hawaiian Shirts, size is now represented by the HTML tags:

<p><b>Large</b></p>

These indicate that the data—the word "Large"—between the tags should be placed on a new paragraph line and show in bold text. But it cannot help the computer understand the nature of the letters and symbols it is representing. To the HTML-run system, it's just another string of characters. XML, on the other hand, is completely literate:

<size>Large</size>

The new code can allow information to be found in a different system, placed in a predetermined location, and given a certain appearance, depending on what category the data falls into. Why is this important? If the posted information is never going to change—or at least change rarely—then HTML does indeed serve its purpose. But what if the information includes quantity levels? Should the IT people have to manually adjust the homepage every time the numbers change? That, of course, is impractical. So far, the only two options have been either to painstakingly write custom programs to transfer the data from one system to another, or simply not to have an online inventory. HTML makes it hard to arrange for an accurate, automatic change of data; XML makes it easy. It is particularly useful to bricks-and-mortar businesses, since they are often tethered to aging computer databases that are light-years from being Internet compatible. When they want to create up-to-date Web sites, it has been tricky for them to integrate their old inventory systems with their online counterparts. Using XML allows for a far more efficient method of data transfer—see Chapter 5 for more details.

Many companies hesitate to try this new language because HTML is still the big standard in Internet programming. That's okay. Even if XML takes control in the next few years, your HTML site will still function, since XML is compatible with HTML. Also, if the information on your Web site is largely static—or not requiring frequent updates—there's no pressing need to rush for the latest language. Nevertheless, you may change your mind in the near future. As e-commerce becomes more sophisticated and virtual stores grow, the need for dynamic content is skyrocketing. Perhaps soon your company will be large enough to incorporate a real-time inventory, or maybe you'll need to incorporate other dynamic data. If this happens, XML will be the best option. When technology is advancing this quickly, it's important to anticipate future needs. Companies that adapt only when backed into a corner are far more likely to fail in cyberspace. So try to find programmers who know XML, especially if you might be using it any time soon.

Outsourcing

Although talented IT employees can help you create a successful shopping site, you'll need to make a separate decision about purchasing. In the first place, it will be hosted on a separate server. Transactions involve the transfer of private data, and so they must take place on a completely secure server. The physical location of that host will in no way affect the site, so the choice of servers is entirely up to your company. Do you want to host purchasing in-house, or outsource to a different company? Despite its well-deserved reputation for eliminating the "middleman," the Internet doesn't always encourage simplification, nor does it mean that your company will no longer require affiliates. Some online services are simply best handled through outsourcing.

Admittedly, it can be tempting to manage the site internally. After all, building the site from scratch does allow you the greatest degree of control. But a purchasing site is far more complicated than the shopping site; it requires special account software that you will probably have to design yourself. You'll also need to observe strict standards in creating and maintaining your own secure server, which requires an extensive and highly trained IT department. Running an in-house purchasing site is a huge drain on resources. In general, it's only a good solution for large corporations that physically require a complex, personalized site.

Smaller companies benefit most by outsourcing some aspect of their online business to an ISP and/or turnkey.

Choosing an ISP

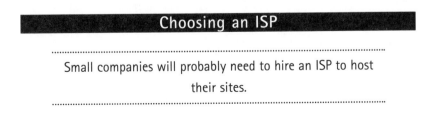

Small companies will probably need to hire an ISP to host their sites.

ISPs, or Internet Service Providers, are a good option. They're the companies that grant large-scale access to the Internet, so they can offer your company sufficient space for your future site. They are fairly flexible, and can grow in size along with your company. More important, if you hire an ISP, it will provide a ready-made secure server and merchant software. Think of them as cyberspace land-lords: They'll rent you the space in a secure environment, but you still get to decorate the rooms as you see fit. It spares you the need to build your own house, which is difficult for companies that are ham-pered by limited resources.

Nevertheless, not all ISPs are created equal. Some are better than others, and you want to make sure that the company you choose is the best for your business. Shop around, and ask lots of questions before you make up your mind. Listed below are some qualities you'll want to look for in an ISP.

Good Hardware

- **Capacity.** Your ISP should have sufficient capacity for your site, including plenty of room to grow. This isn't usually a problem— most ISPs offer at least 10 to 20 MB of storage space, which is quite comfortable for most small companies.

- **Speed.** How fast is the connection? The success of your busi-ness depends on the expedient transfer of information, so you want an ISP that can send or receive data as quickly as possi-ble. This means that the provider should be fairly close to a "backbone," or a main line of communication on the Internet. Think of it as a literal information superhighway. Most providers have to route data through various channels before it reaches the backbone, where it gains entrance at a network access point, or NAP. Each individual detour is referred to as a "hop." If you put all the slang together, you want an ISP that is only a few hops from the NAP. Anything over ten is definitely too many—uploads and downloads on your site would be delayed. Aim for eight or less. Incidentally, this connection, or any connection to the Internet for that matter, can also be referred to as a "pipe."

- **Bandwidth.** Bandwidth relates to the width of the route itself. While hops can indicate time-consuming detours, a limited bandwidth can cause data congestion, which impedes the actual flow of information. This is especially problematic when there is a high demand for your site, which might occur right after a large ad campaign, or just after you open your doors for the first time. Although in general it's nice to be popular, success often comes at a high price: when too many people try to access your page, a traffic jam can occur. This is very bad—the resulting slow pace of data transfer will cause lengthy downloading times. If your Web site takes too long to access, customers will click off your site and look elsewhere. Ironically, then, effective campaigns might actually harm your Web site! Make sure the ISP can handle a high volume of traffic without a sluggish connection.

- **Security.** We saved the most important software requirement for last. Your ISP *must* provide a secure server for all transactions; after all, that's the main reason companies outsource purchasing in the first place. Do some digging to find out exactly what degree of protection they can offer. They should use one of the two standard protocols that enable encryption: either Secure Socket Layer (SSL) or Secure HyperText Transfer Protocol (S-HTTP). It is imperative that you protect your customers' financial information. Make sure the ISP has never experienced any security problems.

Reliability

Pick a reliable ISP. Do a little research to find out how often the server goes down, and how quickly the ISP responds when it does. Be very picky. Successful Web sites must be available 24 × 7—in other words, every hour of every day. From time to time, a server or network will crash, which is known as a "fail-over." Admittedly, there's no perfect ISP. All providers experience occasional problems, but even then they should still be fixed without lengthy delays. Your Web site needs to be supported by a hale and healthy service. Choosing a cheap, obscure ISP is not the best idea. You'll probably have the best luck if you go with a major company—they simply have more resources and more experience fixing problems, which equals a greater reliability.

Software and Other Services

- **Passwords.** Check to see if the ISP's customers are allowed to select and control their own passwords. It's just safer. You don't ever want to be locked out of your own site.

- **Merchant Software.** If the ISP will be hosting your online purchasing site, you'll automatically use their merchant software. Ask about the package they use. What kind of secure server software do they have? Who provides their electronic payment system? Make sure that their software is both quality and appropriate to your own needs.

- **Advertisement.** Most ISPs are willing to promote your site in some fashion, or at least register it with a search engine. Find out how your marketing department can work with the ISP to best advertise the Web site.

E-mail aliases can help your public image. They make your
company seem larger and more professional.

- **E-mail.** Ask the provider what kinds of e-mail services they offer, especially if your business requires frequent communication
  with customers. Good ISPs include e-mail boxes, so that you
  can easily receive messages from both clients and associates.
  This is helpful particularly to entrepreneurs looking for a more
  professional look; they can have an "e-mail alias" address
  posted on the Web site that forwards mail directly to a personal
  box. In addition, you can have other e-mail aliases that send
  messages to specific employees. For instance, you could create
  an alias address, such as helpme@ourstore.com, listed on the
  site for customers who have product-related questions. The
  mail can be sent straight to a designated sales representative,
  who can then provide the customers with info.

- **Data Tracking.** Keeping tabs on customer traffic is an extremely
  important activity. Only choose an ISP that already has the capability or is willing to cooperate with the software package of your
  choice. You'll need to know info like which pages work well and
  which ones don't, so that you can continue to streamline the
  purchasing process. The data can also help your company monitor customer buying patterns and client demographics. For further information on data mining, see Chapter 5.

A Trained Tech Staff

We guarantee that at some point you will have problems with the ISP.
Your site might experience "technical difficulties" or you'll feel confused about a certain detail and need your questions answered ASAP.

When this happens, the ISP tech staff should be your best friend—not the enemy. Try to find a company that provides 24 × 7 support and ask the ISP what kind of training their help-line people receive. You also want to know what *level* of help they are best equipped to offer; if your company largely employs technical novices, you want to receive simple advice—uncluttered by techno jargon. The tech support line should also be adequately staffed, not one guy hopelessly swamped with work. Call their help line a few times to see how long you'll usually have to sit on hold. It should not be longer than five to ten minutes. In an emergency, Kenny G can't solve your problems!

Experience

E-commerce is a brand new field of business. Although new companies are popping up everywhere, many smaller ISPs have little to no experience. Even the older providers have only been hosting sites for a few years. You do *not* want to work with a baby ISP; too many things can go wrong. Instead, focus on the larger national companies. They've been around the block and also have better resources. When making your decision, ask to see a list of their clients, and get in touch with them. ISP customers are often quite willing to talk to you. If they're happy, they want to brag. If they are dissatisfied, they want to share horror stories. Check out the hosted Web sites for quality: How quickly do the pages load? Are any of them nonfunctioning? Again, don't feel stupid about nosing around. Choosing an ISP is an important step, and making a good decision can save your company a lot of future grief.

Price

Try to strike a good balance between price and quality.

Shop around for a good deal, but don't pick a flea-market ISP. By far, the most important consideration is *quality*, not price. If you're serious about your Web site, be willing to pay for a serious ISP. Small start-ups are often enthusiastic and cheap, but they're inexpensive for a reason. They usually don't have the resources and tech record of the big national companies, and if disaster strikes you could wind up paying a lot more than you counted on. Play it safe—and beware of hidden charges. If an ISP has a suspiciously low setup fee and monthly rate, find out what services cost extra, and exactly how much at that.

ISPs are an excellent choice for companies that need to preserve a larger degree of flexibility and independence. Although the ISP provides the resources, your company would still design and handle the purchasing site on its own. It's also really cheap, since you (or your IT people) are still doing most of the work.

Nevertheless, many online businesses lack the funds and manpower to successfully manage a busy Web site if they have to worry about product orders as well. In fact, bricks-and-mortar businesses often have the same problem; after all, order tracking and fulfillment are complex processes. Luckily, there is an alternative. Lots of people find salvation in hiring companies known as "turnkeys" to do the work for them. And, thankfully, this is one real-world solution that transfers beautifully to cyberspace.

The Turnkey Alternative

Turnkeys are companies that accept and process orders, ship products, and perform a variety of other services for retailers. They originally only dealt with offline services like 800 numbers, but many have recently found it profitable to branch out into cyberspace.

What Turnkeys Can Do for You

Turnkey companies can basically run your entire online purchasing site. You'll have to design it yourself, but they will deal with almost anything else. Depending on a variety of factors, turnkeys can provide any combination of the following services; the first two options are those traditionally offered by bricks-and-mortar companies, the rest are offered by newer Internet turnkeys. See which options might work for you.

Traditional Turnkeys

> Turnkeys can help you a great deal if you have limited resources.

1. *Order processing.* If you already work with a turnkey, you know that they will process all your orders for a set price. They'll receive orders, handle customer feedback, and forward the orders to your company for fulfillment. This is a particular boon to small companies, since they often need to reserve their limited time for other, nonroutine tasks. The turnkey should send frequent sales reports to keep their clients updated, and provide detailed statistics and data for your consumption.

2. *Order fulfillment.* For an extra fee, larger turnkeys will also fill customer orders: this includes packing, shipping, and tracking. All you need to do is provide them with the raw product, and they'll do the rest! As with order processing, it's a time-saving service. It allows you and your employees to worry about more pressing issues without neglecting sales service. Consider paying for order fulfillment if your staff is too overwhelmed to accomplish the task quickly and efficiently.

Cyber Turnkeys

Hire an Internet turnkey if you cannot afford
a full-time tech support staff.

Over the past few years, certain Internet start-ups have begun re-defining and expanding upon the turnkey concept. Cyberspace turnkey businesses act a lot like deluxe ISP companies; they handle secure transactions and host your site. But they'll also help you actually construct both your shopping and purchasing pages—and all for a flat monthly fee. They realize that many novice Internet businesses need help developing their online stores, so they provide design templates that enable the user to build Web pages without any knowledge of HTML or other programming languages. The templates not only get a small business online within a few days, but they also help prevent common design mistakes.

These virtual turnkeys will often place you in an online mall, with other companies that use their services. Although many managers balk at being confined to a group of other e-tailers, participating companies can still possess their own URL and domain name. Customers might stream in and out of various stores without even knowing they'd visited a mall! Cyberspace turnkeys are especially popular with individual entrepreneurs, those who lack the know-how and manpower to design and build all the applications on their own.

In addition to getting you online, these companies may even alleviate some of your marketing worries. Since virtual malls depend on their client merchants' success, they'll also usually be willing to register your site with a search engine. The only tasks left entirely to the merchant are site maintenance and order processing and fulfillment—and, as we know, traditional turnkeys can handle these latter two activities.

This might be a good option for the smallest of companies. If you do not employ any Web designers and can't afford to hire any full-time, these turnkeys can make your life a lot easier. Nevertheless, partnering with an online turnkey does detract somewhat from your business independence; it decreases your flexibility and prevents you from building a truly personalized site. Virtual malls, for instance, do not support Intranets or Extranets. If at all possible, you should have your own programmers build the shopping site. You want as much creative control as possible. But whatever you decide, be sure to weigh all the options first—then pick the best course for *you*.

Playing to a Specific Audience

It's impossible to please all the people all the time—you'll have to decide which market is the most important.

Before you begin designing and building your site, you need to know for whom you're creating it. Although most businesspeople think of Web sites as catering only to generic customers, in reality they often serve a broader group that includes new customers, established customers, partners, distributors, suppliers, and a variety of other affiliates. You have to settle on selling to a specific market segment, so you have a solid starting point to commence your work. This is an incredibly basic marketing strategy, yet unfortunately many businesses cast it aside when they begin planning an online venture. Managers know that the Web is accessible to virtually anyone with a computer, so they decide to "broaden" their site by trying to include information for several markets in the one location.

They are, indeed, right about the universal quality of e-commerce. By working online, they will be able to reach a far, far greater population than previously possible. But having a packed house does not mean that your business should abandon its focus. That would be a mistake.

Having a Web site is kind of like engaging in a two-way discussion between the company and a visitor. Effective communication requires clarity and coherence, and those qualities are impossible if your site is trying to carry three threads of conversation at once. You simply do not talk to old customers the way you do with new ones, nor do you treat partners and distributors interchangeably. If you try to *accommodate* every market on your home page, you might only *confuse* every market—and you'll lose business in the process.

So choose one segment. Consider which group will use your Web site the most, and thus merit the greatest part of your energies. Smaller companies have a few different choices, combining various degrees of risk and reward.

Business Affiliates

Gearing the site towards partners or distributors is a good idea if you want to start out in a comfortable situation. You already conduct business with these groups, so a Web site would be just a way to provide better service. You won't make any extra money off of it, though you may save a bundle by cutting operation costs. Think of it as more of an Extranet site than a Web site (see Chapter 5).

Established Customers

This is only a little trickier. Current customers are already familiar with your bricks-and-mortar business, and so they do not need much convincing to shop in your store. They are inclined to trust your service, and are far more likely to buy products than newcomers. Nevertheless, customers are a bit higher maintenance than your business affiliates since the relationship is less formal. You still need to "sell" things, and work hard on presentation. In return, they will generate good revenues, although much of it is merely transferred from the bricks-and-mortar store.

New Customers

Catering to brand-new clients poses the highest risk. They need a great deal of information in order to consider making a purchase, which consequently entails a more elaborate Web site. You will probably need to offer testimonials, detailed product descriptions, your company background, and various other selling points in order to reel them in. It's a lot of work, and also the kind of site most likely to fail. New visitors might not be interested in your services, and older clients might be irritated by a glut of information they already possess. Yet if this approach works, you'll be generating new money—and if you attract enough people, your revenue could skyrocket.

Customer Demographics

If, like most companies, you decide to focus on customers—either new or old—you'll need to break your profile down even further, into demographics. After all, different kinds of people respond to different kinds of advertising. Obviously, not all of your patrons are going to be cookie-cutter images of one another, but you can certainly pick out and address the larger trends. Will your site mainly cater to women? Professionals? Nebraskans? If you haven't already done the research, issue a brief questionnaire to your current customers. As an incentive to complete the form, you can offer a small discount on the day's purchase for each survey returned. There are many different factors to consider.

Age. You shouldn't be overly concerned with specific age—you're more interested in broad ranges. Create check boxes that list categories of age, rather than having them fill in the blanks. Is your target market mostly small children, six to twelve? Teens? Young adults? Seniors?

Gender. This is a pretty obvious one.

Ethnicity. Offer plenty of options, and *always* include a "decline to state" box. You don't want to offend anyone.

Residence. From where exactly are your customers coming? And from what kinds of situations?

Of course, these categories are only a start. You'll want to include other demographics questions that have relevance to *your* store. As you plan, however, you should keep one thing in mind: picking a target market does not mean excluding the other groups. It's merely a starting point. Once you have the main structure of the site inked out, feel free to work in links and information for everyone else. But narrowing your initial focus will prevent the site from becoming cluttered or awkward—like a tree with three trunks. Stick to *one* trunk, then branch out. Organization and focus are crucial to a successful site.

Getting Your Paperwork in Order

Before you go online, you also have to make sure that you obtain all the necessary documents. E-commerce is a serious business. Before the Web "authorities" verify your official merchant status, they will check to see that you have the required legitimacy.

Choosing an Acquirer

....

Obtaining an Internet merchant account can take a long time.
Get an early start!

....

First, you need to shop around for a bank that can handle your Web transactions. Take this step seriously, because your bank plays an important role in your online venture. In addition, the search is actually more complicated than it sounds—just as online transactions are more complicated than traditional ones. In bricks-and-mortar stores, payment generally passes from one hand to another. There's no ambiguity in the transaction, since both parties are clearly agreeing to the purchase. This is good for the merchant, since he receives his money instantly (unless it's a check!), provides the product or services, and all is well.

Online, matters are obviously a bit different. Customer and merchant must interact with one another sight unseen; instead of a meeting, the cyber purchase has been distilled down to a brief, impersonal exchange of sensitive information. Although it's convenient for customers to be able to buy things from their homes, it's still somewhat scary. The Internet at heart is a giant tangle of telephone wires and hard drives. Sending one's private credit information into the void can be very unsettling; most customers know that even mediocre hackers can intercept unsecured messages—including credit card numbers. This is always at the back of a shopper's mind.

Therefore, in order to protect their interests and maintain your own business integrity, your company needs to choose an Internet-savvy bank—in webspeak, an acquirer. Don't go for the cheapest deal. If any security problems were to arise, your business could be in serious trouble. Here are some key qualities you want to consider:

- **The Transaction Process.** Ask the acquirer to run through an imaginary transaction, explaining each step in detail. Make note of what security measures they use and make sure they compare well with other institutions. The bank should also be able to handle transactions in real time, and deliver payments in less than two days. But aside from all that, you just want a solid understanding of their process to help you decide how your business can best respond to online payments.

- **Software.** What kind of software does the bank use? Will it be compatible with your company's own software? Will you need to purchase or lease any expensive equipment? The answers to these questions can help you decide whether that particular acquirer would be a good fit.

- **Price.** Naturally, no banking service is free. They can charge your company in a variety of different ways. You'll definitely have to pay a onetime application fee, which can be hundreds of dollars. There's also monthly fees, charges for leased equipment, and per-transaction fees. These last can take the form of either a flat fee or a small percent of each sale. One thing is for certain—it won't be cheap! Check for hidden add-on costs to ensure that you won't be gouged.

....

Do the research—even if you plan to stay with your bank. You might find a better quality deal elsewhere.

....

When choosing an acquirer, you definitely want to start with your current bank. They're obviously doing a good job, or your company wouldn't be using their services, right? (If you *are* in any way dissatisfied, now's the time to look elsewhere.) Yet even if you love your bank, not all of them offer Internet merchant accounts—and even if yours does, you still need to know the specifics before you sign on. Don't be afraid to take your business elsewhere if you don't feel your company would be getting the best service.

Once you've decided, be ready to wait. Obtaining an Internet merchant account can take up to two months, so don't waste any time postponing this particular task. The bank will eventually issue you a Merchant Identification Number (MID) and a Terminal Identification Number (TIN). These numbers are used by the bank to identify you, both in transactions and in the acquirer's own paperwork. Now you're set to receive payment online!

Digital Certificates

Most Internet customers are profoundly aware of the risks posed by online transactions. They love the convenience of e-commerce, but they also need reassurance that their credit card numbers aren't being misused by a disreputable company or intercepted by clever hackers. A secure server goes a long way towards establishing a safe atmosphere, but there is one more step your company should take: obtain a digital certificate.

A technique known as "spoofing" has made it particularly difficult for a consumer to tell the difference between a legitimate Web site and an illegal front. Someone will register a domain name that is extremely similar to a popular URL—perhaps www.ebey.com. If a surfer accidentally stumbles onto the spoofed site via a misplaced keystroke, she will find a homepage that looks nearly identical to the real deal. Such sites often offer incredible prices in order to lure people in and lull them into a sense of security. If the shopper was unaware of the mistake in the first place, she might shop around and provide credit information to the fraudulent company before realizing the problem. E-commerce security issues like these are currently being prosecuted, but there's still no guarantee. After all, spoofed sites *are* sometimes true businesses that merely want to capitalize on a larger company's success. They may be illegal, but more in a copyright-infringement sense than any real criminal one. All things considered, online security is a vital issue.

> Digital certificates are the best way to assure experienced
> surfers of your legitimacy.

Digital certificates help resolve the problem; they verify that your company is legitimate, possessed of a good credit history, and protected by a specially encrypted bit of code called a "public key." You can apply for a digital certificate with a third-party company like Verisign. These companies will run a thorough background check and inspect your company in person; they will also ensure that you receive a key from the Public Key Infrastructure (PKI). The PKI is an engine that stores public keys; only certificate companies like Verisign have access to it, so they control the gates. This third-party company will perform all of the routine duties before granting your company the desired document.

Customers who want to assure themselves of your reliability can choose to view the certificate from anywhere on the secure server. Having one will bolster your reputation. Just make sure you accomplish all this in advance—as with obtaining a merchant account, this process can drag on for some time. With luck, banks will soon simplify the process by issuing their own certificates.

Setting Goals

One of the greatest pitfalls of e-commerce can actually be resolved before you even get online: You *must* set specific, obtainable goals for the site. Confusion is the business world's greatest enemy, and it can be deadly to any new venture. Unfortunately, many merchants break onto the Web with only the haziest idea of what they expect to accomplish. They treat the venture as either an elaborate experiment or the knight in shining armor, and both of these approaches create a problematic atmosphere.

Remember that some managers want merely to tinker with the Web site. As a result, they often either establish the most nebulous objectives or fail to set goals at all. It's not surprising—if they haven't even decided exactly how to handle e-commerce, how can they predict where it's going? Indecision results in half-measures and contradictory policies, and progress *cannot* occur without direction.

Make sure that you set realistic goals. They are key to maintaining good morale.

The opposite problem is extreme optimism. Some companies convince themselves that e-commerce will immediately double their profits, cure cancer, and halt global warming. An online presence is certainly beneficial, but it's not going to put your company into the *Fortune* 500 overnight. Setting unrealistic goals will *guarantee* a sense of failure, simply because you can't win.

Modest goals are the best option. They provide a solid framework for decision-making and imbue employees with a sense of purpose. The venture will run more efficiently when efforts are focused and everyone works in sync towards a quantifiable end. In addition, the reasonable quality of the objectives makes success likely—and everyone works hard if victory is within sight.

So what kinds of goals should you set? Well, the only definite answer is: Be specific. Whatever aims you have in mind, try to assign them a numeric value. Instead of: "Cut costs," try "Reduce sales costs by 10 percent over the next two years." The first example is too vague to be of any use—the second is concrete enough to serve as a plan.

Other than that, the objectives you set will depend largely on your own strengths and weaknesses, and partly on what market segment you have decided to focus on. Do you want to concentrate on increasing brand awareness? Enlarging the customer pool? Reducing overhead? Improving customer service? It's up to you.

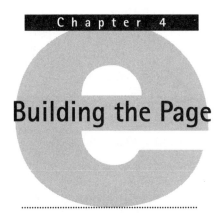

Chapter 4

Building the Page

By this point, you have decided the general focus of your Web site and devised the means to achieve it. Among other things, all of the necessary paperwork is completed, you've staked out a memorable URL, and you've found an experienced ISP or turnkey to host the site. Now you're ready to begin actual site construction. Remember that you should probably hire at least one programmer and/or Web designer for the task unless you are only planning a basic one- or two-page brochure site. Cyberspace is an incredibly visual medium. Since customers cannot touch or actually examine your goods and services, most will by necessity make their decisions based on the general appearance and structure of your Web environment. Image truly is everything in the virtual market. If you post a clear, professional site, you will attract business. However, the sword cuts both ways; few products are strong enough to survive a poorly executed Web page.

Hiring at least one full-time IT employee does not mean that managers will be locked out of the process. On the contrary, they can and should have final say over the ultimate content of the site. After all, they are in the best position to provide a broad perspective and relevant goals. A manager's duty is to bring order to chaos, to ensure that each component merges into a coherent whole. The following six factors affect the quality of your site.

Keep It Simple, Stupid

When in doubt, leave it out!

This is the quintessential rule of e-commerce. Trying to cram a store's-worth of material onto a few virtual pages is a Herculean task—and one that you should absolutely avoid at all costs. A glut of unimportant information creates a cluttered site, which in turn forces potential customers to waste precious minutes digging around. That's bad business. People shop online for convenience, so if your store is inconvenient, they will not hesitate to look elsewhere. Simplicity and clarity help visitors find things with a minimum of fuss; they also help emphasize the information that you *do* provide. Be minimalist. Unless there is a "clear and present necessity" for any one element, don't include it on your page. If you can't explain to *yourself* why that graphic is important, then it's probably not. Chuck it.

The Need for Speed

Web surfer attention spans are notoriously short, largely because they have so many options available in a few keystrokes or one click of the mouse. Our breakneck advances in technology have done wonders for communication. We have the most connected, sophisticated communities in history. Yet ironically, the very immediacy of the Internet has produced a far more impatient shopper. Customers want instant gratification, so online stores that fail to move quickly are likely destined for failure. The push for immediate results means that your pages should load quickly—in ten to twenty seconds on a standard browser. If they are any more sluggish, the average surfer will "click off" and look elsewhere. The need for fast loading is just another reason to create simple Web pages.

Organization

This one is pretty obvious. A confusing site will only annoy visitors. Although nearly all companies intend to produce an organized site, the end result often falls far short of the goal.

The key to successful organizing is in the planning stage. Decide in advance exactly how you want to structure the site. Actually draw a "site map" to aid in a coherent design, and detail the exact location of each page and each link. Customers should be able to navigate in an intuitive manner—in other words, they should be able to make successful guesses about where to find certain items. Don't penalize people for making the "wrong" guess. Frustrated shoppers won't want to stick around: more than half of online customers will leave a badly organized site, regardless of how many other redeeming qualities the page has.

> Use the three-click rule as the guiding formula of your Web site's general structure.

If you can't decide whether the site is self-explanatory enough, use the "three-click rule." All customers should be able to find the data they need within three clicks of having entered the site. Customers should be able to dash in, grab what they need, and dash away again without becoming hopelessly lost. Although four necessary clicks for some links would hardly be a disaster, you still want to keep as close to the ideal as possible.

Reliability

Although your ISP is generally responsible for the stability of your site, you *do* get to choose which ISP to trust in the first place. You also need to know ASAP when the site is inoperative, so you can get immediately on the horn to the help line and fix the problem. If your Web site is down half the time, you'll lose business not only from the blackouts, but from customers who never come back. An online store will only generate money when it's open for business—and if you gain a reputation for frequent crashes, people will stop visiting. Period. Thus at least one employee should be checking the site several times every day. Contrary to popular belief, online stores won't miraculously run themselves.

Be Professional

Your company is only as good as the image it projects.

As the Internet age rolls on, many people have begun to note an increasing disregard for the traditional rules of writing. In casual, nonbusiness communication this is not exactly a huge problem. Your virtual storefront, however, is an entirely different matter. Customers come to your shop to transact business, and it is your job to convince them of your legitimacy. Professionalism actually matters more on the Web than it does anywhere else; after all, in this particular medium, appearance is all-important. Customers usually cannot drive to your store and assess your commitment in person—so if you misspell words or post badly written content, they'll probably conclude that the business itself is haphazard. Provide good customer service and try to project a competent image. You may run this company from your garage, but the shoppers don't have to know it! Likewise, larger companies look extremely foolish when their otherwise impressive Web pages contain typos and poor grammar.

Promote Yourself

On the Internet, it's painfully easy to be just another name in the crowd. After all, that's what literally happens when someone runs a keyword search—you're drowned in a long list of competitors! There are myriad ways to promote your business outside the Web site (see Chapter 6) but don't stop advertising when customers do finally arrive. All of your great service and quality products should impress customers, but you also want to make sure that they keep you in mind for a return visit. That's where brand awareness comes in.

Post your company logo on every page of the site, especially on your main or homepage. If you don't have a logo, invent one. You can do it yourself or get some help from a graphic designer. Pictures are a great way to get people to remember your business—and you want to be the first business they think of when they decide to shop again. You can also support the branding by incorporating any company colors into the main design of the site, just make sure that they aren't so flashy as to be distracting.

All companies should possess these six qualities if they want to run a successful online business. Even if you only want to post a simple, one-page brochure, you still need to ensure an organized, professional result. But for those companies looking to create a true Internet presence, be sure to include the following.

Interactivity

Don't treat your Web site like a standard brochure or catalog—that wastes your singular opportunity to build an *interactive* store.

As we discussed in Chapter 1 of this book, one of the main benefits of the Web has been mass customization. In other words, manufacturers can produce special orders on a large scale. People can go online and assemble their own ideal computer package or build the perfect bicycle from "scratch." These activities used to be nearly impossible, since customers have always been present only after products are assembled and shipped to the distributor. Buying goods and services online is like making a trip to the warehouse and directing the assembly yourself. Since e-tailers' merchandise is often assembled only *after* the customer orders it, the shopper is free to tweak the specifications of a normally standard product. This is an incredibly attractive opportunity for consumers. It empowers them and allows them to become truly involved in the commercial process. And not surprisingly, this unprecedented level of choice is spoiling many consumers to the point where the traditional style of shopping will soon be perceived as inadequate.

Without exception, the best Web sites are those that allow for a certain degree of interaction between merchant and customer. Even if the complexity of mass customization is currently beyond your company's capacity, be sure to include at least some opportunity for customer involvement—even if it's only an e-mail address for feedback. We'll explore more of these opportunities at a later point.

Don't Forget the Cookies!

Personalization is probably the Internet's greatest advantage—it has the power to combine large-scale commerce with specialized contact. Only on the Web can you reach thousands of people while ensuring that each returning customer finds the store uniquely crafted to suit his own tastes. Your online "target market" can actually be a single individual! Personalization, for all the concern about privacy issues, is a huge selling point for nearly all e-tailers. Shoppers usually love Web sites that remember their preferences. Such sites create a friendlier atmosphere and, more important, a convenient shopping experience.

> Cookies let you present a thousand different stores to a thousand different people. Now that's service!

Usually when a surfer visits a large Web site, he is forced to click through pages of irrelevant material before he finds what he needs. Cookie files can remedy the situation. The store merely preserves data from the customer's previous visit, and the next time he passes through, he finds his own interests displayed more prominently. Advertisements, news postings, technical advice, and more can all be specially tailored to each shopper's preferences.

This strategy has panned out brilliantly for many companies; not surprisingly, it takes suggestive selling to an entirely new level! If a cookie reports that Beverly has a fondness for medical texts, then the bookstore's homepage can load with ads for the latest science books rather than the generic *New York Times* Bestsellers list. Without a doubt, Beverly will be a lot more likely to buy something on that trip than if she had needed to dig for titles relevant to her tastes—and that pleases both the company *and* consumer.

Cookies are, admittedly, most often used by larger companies simply because they entail more sophisticated Internet technology. It's quite costly to invest in such tools, and you would also need some sort of IT staff in order to construct the proper secure environment. Nevertheless, cookies are worth the price if your company is willing and able to make a considerable investment in e-commerce.

There is a cheaper, alternative form of personalization: The store can simply have the shopper fill out an online questionnaire and set them up with a customer password-protected account. Every time the customer visits the site, he logs on at the homepage. The store then accesses the pertinent info stored in its *own* database on the customer's previous trips. The drawback of this method is its inherent clumsiness—nobody really likes to take the time to complete the forms, nor do they want to have to log in to every site they visit. The key here, of course, is that it's not as convenient!

Although cookies and on-site forms are currently the dominant modes of personalization, a new technology is just on the horizon. Learnlots.com, a company that provides technical advice to visitors, recently pioneered a function that it calls "Webskin." Learnlots attracts a great deal of traffic by allowing other companies to link to its site. If a customer is surfing at a consulting Web site, then suddenly has a question, he can click through the Learnlots link and land on their homepage. But this is no ordinary homepage—it preserves the exact look and feel of the consulting site the customer just left! The structure, colors, and motifs are all still the same, but the content is decidedly that of the new site. How is Learnlots capable of such a feat? The answer lies in its trademark Webskin. Webskin is a technology that is superimposed over a basic homepage template; when a visitor comes in from a link, the program makes a note of the source and modifies the homepage to look like the original store. It's very comforting to surfers. Instead of feeling shuffled around, they may not even be aware that they're browsing at a new URL. This kind of personalization has incredible potential—eventually, stores will probably be able to use cookie technology to design custom-appearance Web sites for each client. Every visitor would see a homepage designed specifically for her; it would make her feel more comfortable, like a valued client rather than a struggling employee. Although Webskin is not yet sophisticated enough to make this possibility a reality, soon enough such technology will exist.

Shopping Content

The only true rule governing the actual content of your Web site is that there are no hard-and-fast rules. All companies are unique and must decide for themselves exactly what types of pages they wish to build. The structure you choose will depend on your company's particular focus, situation, and the extent of your online presence. Nevertheless, there are certain elements common to most e-commerce sites.

Introduction

All Web sites need a clear structure. Most companies know that unless the site architect provides some form of organization, visitors can become lost in a tangle of disconnected screens. Chaos is certainly not the path to success! So an online store needs a certain page that serves as a table of contents—as the site's main hub. It's usually called a homepage. Homepages are often the first screen customers see when they enter a Web site. Therefore, not surprisingly, their main purpose is to help visitors gain a painless understanding of a store's layout. Any site with more than one or two pages should have a homepage. Include all the contact information for your business, and also offer links to each major area of your Web site. Everything should be arranged in an orderly manner, and it should always provide enough information to answer these three questions:

1. What type of store is this?
2. What kinds of information can I find here?
3. How do I contact this company?

Larger, more complex Web sites may also choose to add a "splash page," which is kind of an introduction to the homepage itself. It provides the company name, logo, and a perhaps a brief statement about the business. A central graphic or phrase then transports people directly to the table of contents. Why bother? Customers may feel a bit overwhelmed if they are first dropped on a complicated homepage. They have to search a crowded screen for the kind of basic information splash pages can offer in a clear, unambiguous format. Splash pages help ease shoppers into your store, so they feel somewhat focused by the time they reach your main page. A good splash page is like a welcome mat—simple but effective.

Once the customers have absorbed your introductory material, your table of contents and/or store map should lead them to other relevant material.

Company History

A company history is supposed to acquaint visitors with your origins and describe how your business has grown to its current stature. Your story serves two purposes: First, it establishes your solid reputation for the uncertain customer. It's a chance to really sell your experience and reliability. Second, it humanizes your business. When you tell customers your company's life story, they are less likely to view you as a faceless, impersonal conglomerate. Both of these factors will make shoppers more willing to buy from you. A company history is particularly important if you're targeting new customers. Existing clients already like your business and don't need much reassurance of your quality. Therefore, if and where you build this screen depends on your own focus.

One word of warning: Avoid getting too personal. Don't use personal pronouns such as *I* or *me,* and don't include information on your personal life, no matter how harmless or flattering. This is usually most tempting to the smallest of companies, who think that a more casual image might create a friendly atmosphere. But don't mistake business relations for friendship; most customers would much rather buy from a reliable, large company than from a nice person working out of her garage. Being too "open" can cost you your professional image. Remember—this is your business, not your tell-all biography.

News Flashes

News flashes are basically any kind of recent information or updates regarding your business and other relevant topics. If you operate a shop that sells antiques, you might post your newest acquisitions or the latest article on wood preservation. Sales or special promotions can also fall into this category—as long as they're recent, they're news.

This kind of information can be partially included on the homepage. Like a movie preview, it can grab a visitor's attention and get him interested in learning more about the topic. Links might then lead shoppers to a "What's New?" page, where they can learn the full story. Sales and other advertisements, alone among Web site content, are pretty much free agents. You can post them wherever they seem most likely to generate interest—anywhere near related items or topics, for example.

The purpose of news flashes is to keep your Web site interesting and dynamic. You want to exhibit a fresh store every day, even if the changes are small. Give customers a reason to return soon; you want them to feel like they'll miss something if they don't visit regularly. You do *not* want customers to see tumbleweeds blowing down the aisles of your virtual store. An outdated page is bad for business. Never be caught showing the banner for a sale that already ended, or products that are no longer in your inventory. The benefits are definitely worth the trouble. Building a solid base of frequent shoppers can really boost your revenue.

Daily updates are the hallmark of a healthy online store.

The Catalog

The catalog is a crucial part of any store that offers online shopping—after all, in order to shop, you have to see the merchandise! Even stores that sell services should include a price list and description of some kind for each service they offer. Not surprisingly, such a list is usually the main focus of the entire store. So don't slap up a haphazard catalog; treat it with the appropriate care.

> Never consider your catalog "final." Always work for a better, more efficient design.

Depending on the number of items you currently stock, you want to group them into a few large categories that can be listed on one screen. That way, customers do not have to scroll down a seemingly endless list of products they don't want. Keep subdividing as necessary—any one grouping should not contain more than ten or so items. If you have an extensive inventory or complicated categories, consider building a search program into the site. That truly minimizes the amount of time customers waste clicking around. They can just type in a desired word or phrase, and all related products show up on the screen. Such a function requires a bit of sophisticated programming, however, so try to make sure you need it. If you only sell twenty kinds of services, a search program would be a waste of time. Always work for the most efficient catalog possible. Be receptive to customer feedback, and fix anything that causes confusion or ambiguity.

Each product on the catalog list should be just a brief name that serves as a link to more information. It streamlines the page and keeps shoppers from slogging through reams of information about products they don't need. Once customers click on a product, a new screen should pop up, providing a detailed description of the product and its specifications. If appearance is a factor (and it usually is), provide a *small* picture of the merchandise next to the description. This way, the page will load quickly but the customer can also see what she's interested in. If you link the small graphic to a full-size photo, the shopper also has the opportunity to wait and view the product in a larger format.

At all times in a catalog, follow this general rule: Only provide detail if the customer requests it. Don't bore him off your site with data he did not ask for. Keep it relevant.

Testimonials

The customer buying process is a delicate mechanism. People consider a variety of factors before they make the decision to purchase a product, and any number of things can sway them along the way.

Matters are even more tricky online, where customers are understandably leery of buying items they cannot see in person. Such hesitation can dampen actual sales, but it also prompts buyer's remorse—which in turn causes that dreaded headache of a high return rate. If you host online purchasing, or even just online shopping, it's in your best interest to do everything you can to help customers feel comfortable and confident about purchasing items from your Web site. One thing you can do is dedicate certain pages to product testimonials.

Testimonials are statements, written by a third party, that support your business and/or products. Lots of them are written by professional critics and other respected professionals—you might want to ask around to see who's willing to evaluate your merchandise. If you operate an antiques store, you could have a reputable appraiser examine your inventory. If she gives you a thumbs up, ask her if she's willing to be quoted on your Web site. Many professionals are willing to write a brief testimonial for free; it's good publicity for *their* business.

Other important testimonials are those that come from satisfied customers. If you establish the proper feedback channels online, you'll probably receive at least a few positive comments. (At least, for your sake we hope so!) Invite your customers to send you their own reviews, and post them. Again, most people will do it for free—they already like you, and besides, being quoted is fun! Just be extremely careful to *always* receive permission before advertising another person's opinion. Also make sure that the reviewer is quoted accurately. Copyright laws do apply in cyberspace, and you don't want to entangle yourself in a messy lawsuit.

So where to put your testimonials? Not in the main body of your site—after all, they *are* only opinion and many people will just not be interested. Anything pertaining to your company in general should be available through a link at the bottom of your company history page: "*Click here* to see what our customers think of us." Specific product testimonials can be linked directly to their corresponding description pages. After reading the specs and seeing a picture of the desired item, customers would have the opportunity to read "customer reviews."

Again, testimonials are a great sales device even if you haven't yet developed online purchasing. People who order your products from the 800 line will have questions and concerns similar to those who order directly from the site.

FAQs

Virtually every online merchant needs to create an FAQ, or Frequently Asked Questions page. If you currently take phone orders, then you know that about 80 percent of customer inquiries touch on the same dozen issues over and over again. If you have a customer help line, you also know that precious hours of production are spent just repeatedly answering these few questions. A FAQ list goes a long way towards alleviating the problem.

You or your sales staff should compile a list of the ten to twenty most common questions that customers ask. You can then craft clear, thorough answers and post both Q & A prominently on your site. One important thing to beware: Do not include endless reams of questions on your FAQ list. This is actually a lot more difficult to avoid than it seems. Sales and marketing people often become so excited about the potential of the project that they begin dumping every question they can think of into the database. That is not the point of a help line. Customers click to the list in the hope of finding a straightforward, quick answer to a particular question. If the FAQ list is too long, it won't be of any use to harried customers. At that point, they'd be better off calling the support line rather than trying to wade through a pile of unnecessary information. If you truly need a complex FAQ page, then you should invest the time in procuring more sophisticated technology for the site. Try including a search function, or organize the questions by category. In short, do everything you can to help customers find the answers they're looking for—and that includes making the information digestible.

So don't forget to create an FAQ page. Unlike many other applications, it benefits both consumer and manufacturer while pleasing your support staff as well. It's a win-win-win situation! Customers are thrilled that their concerns are addressed in a hassle-free manner. Your sales support people are glad to have more time to concentrate on truly complicated problems. And you cut costs while increasing productivity. What's not to like?

Online Support

FAQs will help, but naturally they won't end all customer problems. You'll still need to employ an experienced sales staff. The difference is that now a large part of their focus should shift to online support.

Online support can take a few different forms. The first and most traditional method is to have a special phone number designated as a help line. This works so well because, aside from meeting face-to-face, phone contact allows the greatest level of communication. People can discuss and resolve an issue in a matter of minutes. The only problem is that phone support forces most dial-up customers to get offline in order to use the phone, and many times they'll forget important information while talking to the sales rep. Even worse, they might even give up while still online. Lots of people think it's just not worth the trouble to be on hold for twenty minutes. You should still have a phone support line, because so many people still prefer it, but make sure that it is adequately staffed for the level of demand you experience.

E-mail is a great alternative. It is within your customers' immediate reach, so they are more willing to persist in getting an answer—and thus more likely to buy something. If a customer submits an e-mail question, she doesn't have to sit around twiddling a phone cord; instead, she can live a normal, full life while awaiting a response! Be sure to designate at least one employee to be in charge of e-mail support. If you create a special e-mail address specifically for customer questions, then you can have them all forwarded to a single person. This allows for a greater degree of consistency and it also gives the sales rep some breathing space to investigate the more thorny problems without being placed on the spot by an impatient caller. The luxury of extra time ensures a more correct, more thorough response than an off-the-cuff suggestion extracted under pressure.

In addition to handwritten e-mails (which are ideal) your company might also consider obtaining an autoresponder program. How does an autoresponder work? It's a pretty simple concept, actually. If a customer e-mails a particular address, the program is instructed to reply with a stock response. This also allows you a greater degree of freedom to answer more pressing requests—instead of having to worry about whether or not you already acknowledged the customer's comment, you can rest assured that the autoresponder thanked the customer for her support and indicated a timeframe during which she can expect a thorough response. Autoresponders are not a great idea if all your e-mail addresses are multi-purpose, but if you can set at least one address aside—an alias if nothing else—then an autoresponder can be profoundly effective.

Granted, e-mail lacks the complete immediacy of a phone call, but a full-time support employee should still be able to return answers within a few hours of receiving the question. Regardless of the situation, shoppers should receive some kind of reply within twenty-four hours, even if it's only to inform them that you're working on a solution or answer. If you wait any longer, you risk alienating potential customers.

....

Only consider chat support if you're capable of staffing the room 24 x 7.

....

Companies with enough manpower have one more option: chat support. This method combines the best attributes of phone help and e-mail. It occurs real time, online, and grants customers instant feedback—while still allowing the employee a little time to formulate a good response. Just host a customer support chat room, and assign representatives to monitor it, in shifts, at all times. Midnight shoppers are thrilled to have their needs addressed outside of normal business hours. The relaxed environment is also a good opportunity for support reps to really take the time to help visitors make a decision. The only drawback is that real-time chat support is not always cost-effective. If you decide to go for it, be willing to accept the fact that sometimes the room will be inactive. You should probably use chat support only when your online store is busy enough to ensure a good amount of traffic in the room. Also, you can poll customers to see if they'd be willing to use the application in the first place. Finally, make sure you post the chat room link on every page. No one can take advantage of this wonderful feature if nobody knows it exists!

Forms

Interactivity entails some level of feedback from your visitors. If you desire a high-quality site, you'll need the ability to accept online information. Still, the way in which you solicit this data is up to your business; you might choose to offer brief surveys in the shopping area of the site, or perhaps allow customers to personalize the merchandise in some manner. These fields—that is, any spaces wherein visitors can enter data—are called forms. They're useful devices, and if you host online purchasing you'll *have* to provide them, even if just for the customer's address and contact information. There are several kinds of forms, any combination of which you can use in your Web site. Listed below are the most common.

- **Input Boxes.** These are the least complicated of types. The name is fairly self-explanatory. They're basically empty fields that can receive any matter of typed customer input. Use them if you're asking the visitor for a free response answer in which there are no predetermined choices or where there are so many options that any other form would be impractical. Input boxes work well if you're asking for someone's name or if you're providing a suggestion box.

- **List Boxes.** If the possibilities are a bit more limited, you might consider having your IT people provide list boxes. These are the narrow, empty-looking forms with a down-arrow button next to them. If you click on the button, it'll open a list below the actual field; you simply select *one* of the choices and click on it. The previous blank form should now contain the chosen word or phrase. It's nice that there's less chance for a visitor to accidentally enter invalid information—like the wrong abbreviation for a state. You can't mail a package to Smallville, MU. Still, since there's no opportunity for the customer to add to the list, you must be careful that all possible options are contained in the field. Otherwise you'll send someone away cranky. Use these for product choices (What color?), shipping preference (Overnight or regular Ground?), and other such questions.

- **Check Boxes.** Use them if the number of choices is even more limited but the customer is allowed to select more than one option. The boxes usually show up as empty squares next to the preprinted choices. You simply click one or more of the empty boxes, and the program records the item(s) as having been chosen. These are great for "Which of the following . . ." questions or requests that the visitor "Please check all that apply."

- **Radio Buttons.** These are the only common forms with a strange name. Radio buttons actually don't have anything to do with broadcasting—they received their name from their resemblance to the little tuner knobs on stereos. Anyhow, radio buttons are just like check boxes, except you can only select *one* item in the list. They're basically just empty circles—when you click on one, a dot appears in the center. If you try to pick a second choice, the dot will disappear from your previous selection.

Although well-informed managers should be familiar with the various options, it's wise to let the marketing people design the actual form itself. They'll have the best idea of what questions to ask and what types of surveys or questionnaires will be most successful. They can then pass it on to a programmer, who will build it and get it online. Before anything is posted, however, take a look at the finished product. Make sure that the forms are clear, direct, and relatively brief. No visitor should have to spend more than a few minutes filling out virtual paperwork.

Privacy Policy

Last but not least, somewhere on your site you should have a page dedicated to describing your customer privacy policy. You can outline your security procedures, assure customers that you never sell or lend client mailing lists, and include any other information that will assure the shopper that their personal data will be kept confidential. You might include the link to this page at the top of your homepage, where it will be readily visible to new customers. If you combine a well-written company history with a good privacy policy, you'll go a long way towards reassuring hesitant customers of your reliability. Again, because they cannot see your company in person, this sort of information is incredibly important.

Tips for Your Online Shopping Site

Don't Hide Information

Your Web site should be as blatant as possible. Some of this depends strictly on good organization, but a lot also rests on the placement of elements within each page. Take a hint from news companies: Important newspaper headlines are always placed near the top of the front page so that they can be easily seen when the paper is folded in half. Similarly, on the Internet, the info on the visible part of a page when it first loads is called "above the fold." Whenever it's possible, keep your most important information at the top of the screen. If your Web page must be longer, then make sure that the only obscured information is a continuation of stuff the customer can already see at the top. Don't bury your important icons at the bottom of the page. If your shopping cart symbol is tucked away in a lower corner, some customers might be unable to find it and simply conclude that your company does not offer that particular service. Your menu bar should also be at the top—your customers should be able to tell immediately which services you can provide.

Writing for the Internet

As mentioned previously, good grammar and correct spelling are key to a professional image. But don't stop with mere adequacy—there are certain *types* of writing that work better than others on the Internet. Good offline writing and good online writing are two very different things.

In the first place, you want to be as concise as possible. Use a minimum of semicolons, dashes, commas, and other forms of punctuation. Good online text is easily "scannable"; customers should be able to get the gist of a passage in less than thirty seconds. When you're online, grammatical simplicity is as important as design simplicity.

Other than brevity, you should also stick to active voice. Avoid passive sentences, since they fail to provide an energetic image. Which one of these sentences is more effective?

- Our Web page can be accessed by clicking on the left-hand button.
- Click on the left-hand button to access our Web page.

The second sentence presents a clearer, more assertive image. Active language helps maintain interest; customers are more likely to stick around at a dynamic site. If your language puts them to sleep, you didn't do your job correctly.

Avoid Long Paragraphs

It can be very tempting to treat online sites as interchangeable with real-life modes of communication. It's also a serious mistake to do so.

Countless businesses move online without thoroughly considering the differences between these two media; they simply copy the material from their regular pamphlets or brochures and post it on the new Web site. Granted, that *is* the most efficient method, but it's also not the path to a successful online store. Many styles and techniques that work in print just do not translate well to cyberspace. One of these is the use of traditional paragraphs.

Posting lengthy prose online is usually a good way to repel potential customers. This is partly because Web shopper attention spans are so very short. People are becoming accustomed to the incredible speed of the Internet, and they want all of their online business to match the frenetic pace. It's the TV channel surfer mentality: "If I'm not interested within seconds, I'll look for greener pastures." You must draw them in immediately or lose them. The other argument for brevity is that it's simply more difficult to read things online. Information must be packed into a fairly limited space; when a page of even normal length loads, the viewer must scroll down to see the end, thereby losing sight of the top. This inability to see the document as a coherent whole degrades overall continuity. It's just one more reason why, whenever possible, you should try to keep your most important material above the fold.

In order to avoid long paragraphs, stick to the bare bones. Only include sentences that contribute vital information; anything else should be thrown out. Don't write essays—they'll likely be too bulky for online consumption. Break your passages into easily digestible pieces. Describe your product in more of an outline format.

The best way to produce effective online prose is to use bullet points. They function almost like little flashing neon signs, showing the reader where each key point is located. They make page-skimming quicker and more productive. Which one of these examples is a faster read?

A. Internet businesses are becoming increasingly savvy. Many of the first companies to venture onto the Web adhered largely to traditional brochure guidelines. They initially failed to take advantage of the interactivity permitted by the new medium, but having heard the surfers' clamor for more input, they are now providing for customer feedback. In addition, Web companies are learning to use graphics to the best effect, and they're starting to really enjoy the use of animated text.

B. Internet businesses are becoming increasingly savvy.

- Older companies failed to implement interactive functions.
- Due to complaints, they now provide for customer feedback.
- Online companies are increasingly proficient with graphics.
- These businesses are also using animated text.

Just be careful not to include too much explanation for each bullet point; they shouldn't carry more than three or four lines of material. If you need more space, you can always add a "Click here for more information" link. That way, interested readers can still learn more—but everyone else isn't stuck scrolling past material they don't care about. Clarity is key.

Get Rid of Your "Civilian" E-Mail Address

Putting your personal e-mail on your business cards is rather like including your home address. It's a bit rinky-dink.

When customers explore your online store, they need to be assured of your reliability and success—and they won't buy anything unless they see outward signs of these two qualities! In particular, small companies should make a special effort to project that all-important professional image. That includes everything, even down to their e-mail address. A regular personal address, like mike@aol.com, makes your business appear rather amateurish. You want to avoid the garage-business aura at all costs. Take the time to purchase a domain name for your e-mail system; it's definitely worth the price, because it lends your business a more authoritative air. Mike@mystore.com is a vast improvement. If you still want to receive business mail in your private box, you can always use an e-mail alias for the online storefront. If directed, the system will simply forward all the mail from a particular address to your own box.

Text Effects

• **Font.** What types of fonts should you use? There are tons of styles available to the user—so many, in fact, that it's hard to choose. As with most online special effects, moderation is key. Experiment with a few different fonts to see which ones offer the best image for your business, then adhere to one or two choices. Using five or six fonts throughout your site is a bad idea—it makes the pages appear disorganized. Your Web site is supposed to look clean and unified. No customer will be impressed if confronted by a veritable bouquet of Times, Courier, Book Antiqua, and six other typefaces. On the contrary, they'll probably just be annoyed. With its numerous pages and links, a Web site is difficult enough to organize. Consistency serves as an important binding element. Oh, and one more thing: Stay away from cursive fonts. They rarely add any true benefit, and they are harder to read. If you *must* include cursive, try to confine it to a large-print title.

- **Underlining.** Never underline normal text. On the Internet, such an effect virtually always indicates that the word or phrase serves as a link to a different page. Using it for other purposes will frustrate and/or confuse a lot of potential customers. Don't do it. Try bold or italic text for emphasis.

- **Color.** One of the more fun text effects is color. In paper-based pamphlets and flyers, you're normally stuck with a monochrome look. Additional colors for the text are expensive. Your Web site, however, can be a bit more cheerful at no extra charge. You can use red or other vivid hues to highlight key words and phrases, or maybe blue to represent all your links. Still, you do want to pick a major color and stick with it for most of the text. If your Web pages look like giant rainbows, they'll be dazzling but hard to read. Also, stay away from yellow. It doesn't show well on the screen.

- **Animation.** Animated text is a brand new option. Before the Internet, it wasn't even really available. So what is it? Animated words can shift or change in almost any predetermined fashion; they can grow, glow, shrink, flash, or appear to roll over, among other things. Animated text is a surefire way to grab a customer's attention, so it can be quite useful. Sales and other promotion boxes that employ such effects are more likely to attract business. As usual, just be careful not to go overboard. A ton of flashing, dancing words looks tacky, and might very well give the reader a headache. Don't let your Web site turn into the Las Vegas Strip!

Choosing Graphics

Graphics are very useful when employed properly. On the most basic level, they brighten up a plain Web page and provide a certain level of interest. But they play many roles beyond mere aesthetics. Posting the company logo, for example, is a great way to reinforce your business's identity and ensure that customers remember your site. In addition, if you sell a product in which appearance plays a large role—say, vintage bikes—then you'll want to provide pictures to aid customers in their decision. Small inserts like the ubiquitous click-through "shopping cart" graphic can also ease the transition between pages without adding a lot of written clutter.

Nevertheless, graphics can do a lot of harm when used in a careless fashion. Customers want to accomplish their task quickly and with a minimum of fuss; nothing will annoy them more than to be hindered and confused by a graphics-encrusted page. Since pictures require a longer amount of time to download, an overabundance of them can significantly delay the shopping experience. Visitors will become irritated and predisposed to dislike your product. But beyond the time delay, jumbled graphics can ruin a page. Remember that simplicity is the governing principle of web design. With eight flashing banners and twice as many icons, it becomes very difficult for the customers to find what they're looking for—and they know perfectly well that another, perhaps clearer site is only a few clicks away. When you do include graphics, keep them as minimalist as possible. The less detailed your company logo, the faster it will load.

> When it comes to graphics, *moderation* is
> the best rule of thumb.

Warnings aside, you still almost certainly want to include some images. Yet choosing what kinds of graphics to include can be a bit tricky. If you're only going to use them sparingly, then you want to pick really good quality images. But which ones? Computer graphics can generally be broken down into a few broad categories: functional, cartoon, and photo. When making selections for your site, remember to err on the side of simplicity; if you don't truly need it, don't use it.

- **Functional Graphics.** Functional graphics exist merely to grant your company a more professional image. They are composed of geometric shapes or other abstract components—most of them are used to decorate the site, not convey information. They include generic buttons, boxes, lines, and other figures that you might need in order to create a dynamic Web page. Logos are an important subcategory of functional graphics. Although most trademarks retain the characteristic simplicity of the group, they do more than just adorn the site. They represent your company. We see examples of successful logos nearly every day—despite being deceptively basic in form, they are incredibly effective. For example, the Nike swoosh isn't actually a picture of anything; it's just a simple, evocative shape. Yet it's vitally important to Nike's company image. Because of clever marketing, the swoosh has become highly identified with a particular shoe manufacturer. The same can be said for the Disney mouse ears logo. It's amazing how three overlapping circles are understood immediately, around the world, to represent a mouse—and by extension the company itself. Remember that your ability to create brand awareness depends on having a simple way to identify your company. And, no matter what kind of site you have, you'll need *some* sort of functional graphics, even if just to use a few arrows or borders. Companies that sell an intangible product or service will especially rely on the ability to represent themselves in an appropriately abstract, formal manner.

- **Cartoon Graphics.** The name of these graphics is pretty self-explanatory. They include drawings or sketches that form pictures of people, places, and things. Cartoon graphics are more accessible than functional ones; they are often best used in conjunction with stores that want to establish a nonthreatening atmosphere. Since cartoons are created by hand, they generate a casual tone and place the customer at ease. They can be humorous, as in the comics, but they can also be used in a practical manner. Either way, they're the most user-friendly of the three types. But they're not always the best option. Whether or not you choose to employ them depends on the image you wish to project: Legal offices normally opt for a serious mien and thus use functional graphics instead. After all, charming cartoon lawyers would hardly inspire most customers to patronize the firm. It's too chummy for the situation. A pet store, on the other hand, needs to create a warmer, more personal image. You wouldn't normally feel comfortable buying a puppy from a faceless conglomerate! Drawings of dogs on your homepage will be more effective than a minimalist graphic—and they also load more quickly than photos.

• **Photo.** Many businesses need complete realism in order to survive. If you sell bicycles, for example, drawings of the different models will not suffice. Quite understandably, few customers will trust your cartoons enough to shell out $200 for an unseen product. People would rather go to a store and see the bike in person; convenience can only account for so much. A few snapshots, on the other hand, can provide some assurance that the bicycle is a desirable item. (A good return policy can do the rest.) Photographs are best used for e-tail stores that sell a tangible product. If you're a plumber, you probably don't need Kodak prints to explain the company; in fact, a close-up of corroded, clogged pipes might prompt customers to stay away in droves. Booksellers also usually work best with just functional and/or cartoon graphics. But an arts and crafts store *must* exhibit photos to sell the work. Although pictures make take longer to load, they are simply nonnegotiable in many cases. Just make sure that you do really need them—and know that if you're going to use photographs, make sure that they are high quality. This will be discussed further in just a moment.

So where can you obtain your graphics? Start by looking online. You can actually download any isolated graphic that you encounter—provided that it has not been copyrighted by the creator. It sounds easy, but unfortunately, the copyright condition is a lot more restrictive than it seems: You usually can't tell if the average graphic is protected or not. Unless the image has a notice or copyright symbol (©) showing on the screen, it's incredibly difficult to tell if the designer has registered her creation. A few people will print reproduction permission if they want to allow free use of the graphic, but most do not. Therefore, to be on the safe side, you should always assume that an average, unmarked image *is* copyrighted, and you should not download it without the express permission of the creator.

Fortunately, there are dozens of specially designated sites on the Web where you can either download free graphics or pay for the privilege; some sites even offer packages, so that you can choose from a convenient bank of graphics. At these Web sites, you can pretty much find anything you need, whether it's simple elements such as buttons or arrows or detailed pictures. If you shop around, you might find some excellent clip-art for use on your Web site—and if you download these, you might not need to hire an expensive graphic designer to create your images! Of course, there's always a trade-off. Anything you download will, by definition, not be original work. If you truly want a unique look for your Web site, you're probably better off creating your own graphics. Everything depends on what you need, tempered by what you can afford. And don't go nuts at the graphics sites; people often become so involved in the shopping process that they load too many images onto their Web pages. It's somewhat akin to going to the grocery store when you're really hungry! Be smart and make a shopping list. Decide in advance exactly what number and type of pictures you need—and then stick to the plan. That way, you can look around in a more sensible manner.

Once you're ready to download, there are still a few things you should know in order to be conversant on the topic. HTML files, or files that normally contain text, cannot be used to effectively transmit graphics. Photos and illustrations are far more complex than text—too complex, in fact, to orchestrate a standard file transfer in a reasonable amount of time. After all, a run-of-the-mill graphic can involve over *fifty times* the amount of data that an HTML file contains. In essence, trying to download them full-sized would be like trying to shove the proverbial camel through the eye of a needle. So, in order for graphics to have any practical use on the Internet, programmers had to find a way to "shrink" the files for transmission. They soon developed file formats made specifically to compress graphic images to a manageable size. By far, the two most common formats right now are GIF and JPEG.

Graphics Interchange Format, or GIF, is the more basic system of the two. In response to a download request, it shrinks common graphic files into a streamlined, 256-color package. The Web browser reads the compressed file, then enlarges and displays it on the Web page within seconds. Unfortunately, the efficiency of the process involves a trade-off: Although the high level of compression results in a quicker download time, the resolution is not very sharp. GIF files thus work best with functional or cartoon graphics, or other images that contain a lot of solid colors. Basic logos and drawings simply do not require a wealth of detail to be effective, and they benefit greatly from a faster transfer speed. One version of the GIF format, 89a, even allows for a brief animation effect; it can display a few different images in rapid succession, thus creating the illusion of movement.

Some graphics require a better-than-average resolution. If you sell certain types of products—like technical items or clothing—shoppers will want to see high quality photos. In these cases, the GIF format just doesn't cut it; blurry images can irritate your potential customers. They want detail! In order to satisfy more rigorous standards, programmers have developed an alternative to GIF files: You can also use the Joint Photographic Experts Group (JPEG) format. The capabilities of this process are simply astounding; instead of the

GIF's comparatively paltry 256-color palette, the JPEG format can support about *16 million* different colors! JPEG files can produce an incredibly high-definition image. Photographs that involve delicate hues or fine details are well-served by the process, which is a real boon to e-tailers with visual products. Of course, there's the inevitable hitch. JPEG's complex graphics cannot be compressed as well, and therefore can take several minutes to load, depending on the resolution of the image and the speed of the user's modem. It's a good idea to use the lowest effective level of resolution, since loading speeds are far more important to the average customer than sharp photographs. Usually only die-hard techies are willing to wait longer than thirty to sixty seconds for a page to show.

Obtaining graphics from other sources is often a good idea, since it is relatively painless and usually inexpensive. Nevertheless, there's another way to add photos or drawings to your Web site. Instead of downloading images from the Internet, you can create them and scan them in yourself.

Scanned Photos

Getting your visual aids from other Web sites may be easy, but remember that such convenience comes at the price of originality. And anyhow, it's not always possible to obtain all of your graphics from elsewhere in the first place. If you need to display product photos, you're probably not going to find suitable material on somebody else's homepage. Instead, you have to procure and scan the photos in yourself. The good news, at least, is that you won't have to worry about infringing on someone else's copyright. You just have to make sure that you take the proper steps to ensure the quality of your photos or personal sketches. Drawings are usually fairly easy to deal with—they're less complex than photographs, and scan well into most computers. Photos, however, necessitate more care. When you begin the scanning process for a photograph, you'll want to keep the following advice in mind.

- **GIGO.** Garbage in, garbage out. The old computer maxim holds very true when it comes to scanned pictures. Accept this fact: The picture that loads on your Web site *will* be poorer quality than the one you scan in. Even the most complicated Xerox machines can't improve on original documents, and neither can even the most high-tech scanners. So you need to pick a really good photo to serve as the original. This is not always as easy as it sounds. In the first place, use pictures with a sharp focus; anything that starts out fuzzy or blurry will only look worse once it arrives online. For the same reasons, beware of photos taken in low light or of distant objects. Also, recall that small photo sizes enable faster loading; as a result, you'll also want to reduce the dimensions as much as possible. So the vicious trade-off once again rears its ugly head: Since shrinking a picture negatively affects resolution, try to choose pictures with a minimum of detail. A clean, clear, simple image is best for all Web sites. With everything you post, stay as close as you can to these ideals. Since these conditions can be very difficult to fulfill, try to arrange for a professional to handle the photos. Don't post amateurish snapshots, or your company will appear just as slipshod.

- **Scanner Resolution.** Photo resolution is measured in dpi, or dots per inch. The dots refer to pixels, which are the tiny points of color that make up an image. The higher your dpi, the sharper the picture will be. Try to avoid posting pictures with an extremely low dpi—they won't turn out very well. This does not always depend on the quality of the actual photo; a lot has to do with the scanner you're using; if it's a second-rate machine with a low resolution, your Web photos will probably appear grainy or blurry no matter how great the original was. Unfortunately, you have to walk a pretty thin line. Using a huge, expensive scanner is probably a bad idea, too! Most browsers are set to load pictures as efficiently as possible, and remember that speed sometimes precludes quality. If you scan in a really great photo at, say, over 1000 × 1000 dpi, that same great photo might delay the page load for a few minutes. Even more important, a lot of customers won't have the high-tech applications necessary to even appreciate the quality in the first place. If your site absolutely requires large, high-resolution photos, put them on their own special pages. The main traffic areas can then post a clickable, thumbnail-sized version as an optional link. As a result, customers will then be able to *choose* if they want to wait the prescribed amount of time to see the full-size photo. Never hold your visitors hostage to a long loading time. Since using a scanner for photos can be so tricky, you should consider purchasing a digital camera if you'll be taking the site photos yourself. (See "Digital Cameras," below.)

- **Don't Dither.** To keep your pages loading quickly, you can also limit the number of colors used in the photo. First, as a rule, the more intricate your palette, the longer it will take to download. Also, many computer displays are only capable of reproducing a small number of absolute colors—which means that the benefit of having a JPEG file that can reproduce, literally, 16 million different shades is worthless if the monitor can only handle a few dozen. What's worse is that monitors will try to adapt to the file colors, with regrettable results. When confronted by an unfamiliar tint, they'll expand on their own range by "dithering," which means that they mix individual colored pixels to imitate new hues. This can look really poor if the pixels on a customer's monitor are large; instead of rich, smooth colors, they'll see a confusion of visible dots. It's like looking at a Monet painting from two inches away. If the colors in your desired photo are so delicate as to prompt dithering, choose a more basic photo! The only exception is if you know that the majority of your customers have the proper equipment.

Digital Cameras

Digital cameras are devices that take pictures without the use of film. Instead of chemically imprinting an image onto a roll of Kodak, digital cameras either save the image onto a computer disk or store it as a file in the camera's memory. There are several benefits to this method.

In the first place, you don't need to develop the photos—they're finished in the instant the shutter clicks. You can then simply plug the camera into your computer and download the picture files. They can be displayed on the screen within seconds! Such a fast process means that you can really take the time to get the pictures just right— you won't have to run the film to a developer every time you want to see how the photos are turning out. With a digital camera, you can view the results of a shoot, decide how to improve them, make the necessary adjustments, and reshoot all within a few minutes! Not only is this highly efficient, but it's easier for you to wind up with a high quality result.

Additionally, since the photo files are downloaded directly into your hard drive, there's no need to run the photo through a scanner, which will necessarily degrade the picture quality. The more times you copy an image, the less distinct it becomes—so if you can skip a step along the way, go for it!

If your company won't be taking the pictures itself, a scanner is still the only option. Otherwise, you should probably buy a digital camera. After all, scanners can get the photo online, but the quality won't be the greatest; a digital camera is truly the best way to get sharp, clear photos onto your homepage.

Audio and Video

The rules for incorporating audio and/or video into your Web site are similar to those for graphics: be sensible. If anything, however, such devices should be used even *more* stingily than pictures. Your most complicated graphics can be an inconvenience to many customers, but all they really need to solve the problem is a fast modem. And happily, as technology progresses, more and more people have a decent version. The once-ubiquitous 14.4 speed is now practically a fossil. Conditions are improving so quickly largely because the universal need for good quality modems is so obvious. Anybody who has ever had to wait for a sluggish page to download can appreciate the value of a better modem! To this end, most computer packages now come standard with the fastest modem available, so new surfers don't need to actively seek out the necessary technology.

Audio and video, however, are a completely different story. In order to fully appreciate the merits of a web video or live broadcast, customers need to have specific plug-ins, which do *not* come standard with the average computer set-up. Even once they get home, most Web surfers still do not see the need to download or buy plug-ins. For one thing, at the present, they are only useful on a small percentage of Web sites. That will eventually change, but most Web sites currently do not offer special audio or video technologies. People are also especially put off by the lengthy downloading time necessary for most video or audio files. In order to experience most clips, visitors have to be patient enough to wait around for several minutes to see them. Lots of consumers just see it as too much trouble for too little benefit.

So what exactly are plug-ins? They're special programs that enhance the capabilities of your browser. You can download them, usually for free, on the Internet from companies like Netscape. They allow you to view special files and effects that a basic browser cannot: streaming video, live broadcast audio, and specially formatted text files—like actual brochures. These capabilities are most useful to companies that truly need them in order to effectively market their products. Music stores, for example, might find it difficult to sell music unless the shopper can listen to it first. A man who videotapes weddings might want to post clips of his work, so that customers can feel reassured about the quality. Yet although plug-ins can be incredibly helpful, you should still use them sparingly. If your entire Web site centers around video or audio clips, a lot of otherwise interested customers may become disenchanted and leave.

The key is to be very careful about how you display such media. Offering it as an option is not a bad idea, especially if the clips or broadcasts are particularly relevant to your business. But don't go overboard. Don't let the customers feel like they'll need plug-ins to shop. Special technology should be peripheral, a bonus. Know your target market, and whether it's tech savvy or more mainstream; a Web site that centers on the latest technology will alienate the average surfer.

Syndicated Content

It's incredibly important for online stores to present a fresh face to the world each day. In order to maintain a solid following of customers, vendors must show a compelling reason for visitors to stop by. If a shopper visits your store and has a positive experience, she'll likely browse again in the near future. But let's say that she goes back to your store a couple days after her first visit, and everything is identical; the store has not changed one whit. Your customer will probably be a bit disappointed. If she returns later and your store is still a carbon copy of the original trip, she might very well depart permanently for greener pastures. People are attracted to novelty, especially online. Although certain bricks-and-mortar stores might survive with an aura of consistency, Web surfers desire constant change. If you fail to spend quality time ensuring that your store receives frequent updates, you'll lose a lot of business.

The problem, of course, is that it's difficult for small companies to allocate such large chunks of time and resources to the Web site. Managing an online store is a full-time job—and it requires a full-time effort, often by more than one person. Many Webmasters feel overwhelmed. Although new material may initially be an easy task, after a certain period of time it becomes difficult to generate interesting tidbits every single day. Yes, it is certainly possible to just update the site on a more infrequent basis, which is what most small stores do. Yet a stale homepage will cost you some daily or near-daily customers: If you can't hold their interest, somebody else will! Luckily, there is a simple way for the smallest companies to create and maintain novelty. Your Web site can procure syndicated content.

Syndicated content is material that you "lease" from other companies. You might be charged a small fee for the privilege, but many syndication businesses will merely require you to provide links to their own site. Syndication offers your company a wide variety of content, from comics to news flashes. Your company simply chooses which elements it wants to incorporate into the page, then processes the request with the syndication company. After you have obtained permission, you download the bits of HTML code that correspond to the components you have selected, and voila—you have fresh material, every day. You don't even have to update it yourself; it changes automatically!

> Syndicated content is only effective if it's something your target market will be interested in.

If you decide to include syndicated content in your store, try to place it on your homepage, where visitors can easily see it. Do your best to keep the topics relevant to your customers' interests. A small service company might decide to include frequent updates on the local weather; office supply businesses can offer stock quotes or brief management advice; toy stores can post daily cartoons or puzzles; hobby/sports stores might offer articles on various pastimes; health food stores can even post a fitness tip of the day! New content, when it's good quality, can generate a regular clientele for your store. Your site will never stagnate, yet you can focus your energies on the more infrequent but in-depth updates for the actual store. Just remember that syndication does not absolve you of the need for site maintenance—it merely eases the burden!

If you're considering incorporating some outside material, you first need to investigate the various vendors. iSyndicate is the largest and most popular site, but it lacks the flexibility of many smaller companies. Make sure you research the following questions:

1. *What are the terms of the deal?* Find out how much they charge for their services, if anything. Companies that offer free material will almost always require you to provide links to their own site. This can draw traffic away from your own site, so be sure to weigh the possible risks. On the plus side, some syndication companies are willing to pay you a commission for every sale made to a customer who came from your store. Although you'd still rather have customers buy stuff on *your* site, it eases the hardship. Besides, many of the errant customers will eventually return.

2. *Is it easy to customize the format?* Fitting prefabricated material into an established Web page is extremely tricky. Make sure that the company you contract with has provided for quick size and placement adjustments. You don't want the syndicated stuff to dominate your own Web site; it should be a member of the cast, not the prima donna. Make sure that the size is appropriate and that the colors blend well with the company material. You want to have as much control as possible over the presentation—don't let the other vendor run the show.

3. *How reliable is the company?* You ask this question of all your business partners, and you should ask the syndication company, too. But don't necessarily take their word for it. Contact some of their customers and see what they have to say about the experience. Be wary of sites that crash frequently, in which case the

normal "tip" area will exhibit only a lovely gray nothing. The company you decide to work with should be willing and able to uphold its responsibility: new, quality content every day.

Only use syndicated content if you lack the time
to post your own frequent updates.

However helpful syndicated content might be, it's still not a perfect solution. In the first case, it's not unique to your store. Don't forget that those jokes you've been posting could be on several other Web sites worldwide. In the same vein, syndicated content lacks complete personalization—the information that you provide will not pertain specifically to your company. No matter how good the material may be, your own content is always better. The best rule of thumb is to honestly examine the capabilities of your business. If you can manage frequent updates without outside help, then do it yourself. The quality will be superior, because it'll be targeted specifically at your customers. If, however, you find it difficult to post fresh material nearly every day, then try incorporating syndicated content. Don't risk losing repeat traffic!

Don't Be Too *Cutting Edge*

Although being at the forefront of technology is exciting, it's not always the best idea when you run an online store. Recall that most customers will be a few years behind the latest advances, so you should try to use only middle-of-the-road technology on your Web site. Assume that the customers' modems will be mediocre and that they won't have downloaded the latest plug-ins—perhaps because they're not even able to. Some browsers will and some won't be able to host fancy plug-in capabilities, so to be on the safe side, assume that your customers will be working with a simpler, older browser version. Unless your clientele is mainly the techie crowd, your site won't be harmed much by relatively traditional effects. Focus on a brilliant, unique design, not gadgets.

Eliminate Dead Links

Part of your regular site maintenance routine should be checking for dead links, which are connections to Web sites that are either closed or in a new location. When someone clicks on a dead link, the computer will fail to find the appropriate site and display an error message. This is obviously not good! You do not want customers to be shunted off to a problem screen when they're trying to reach a related site. Naturally, with your internal links this isn't usually a problem, since it's easy to keep tabs on your own status. But dead links can quickly crop up if you don't frequently test your links to other Web sites. If a partner or competitor goes offline or changes their URL, you need to know about it ASAP; the partner companies will probably inform you immediately, but competitors might not. So it's up to you and your IT staff to make the rounds on a regular basis. Failure to do so will result in a substandard site. Even though exterior links do not directly pertain to your store, they do contribute to a customer's image of your overall quality. Having a few dead links is like publishing a telephone directory with wrong phone numbers and addresses—utterly careless.

Navigation Help

It's relatively simple for customers to get lost in your Web site—that means they've decided to retrace their steps or reach a different application, but they're not sure where to go. Usually, just allowing them to back up or jump straight to the homepage will solve the problem, but you do have to offer those options in the first place! Include site directions on *every* page—which includes having at least a "Back" and "Return to menu" button. Put them at the top, above the fold, so that they're easy to spot. This will help prevent customers from falling into dead ends. Also provide a site map option, so that visitors can get a clear picture of exactly where they are, where they want to go, and how to get there. A site map is a clear outline of the pages on your Web site. It has the homepage and/or splash page at the top, and then branches out like a topic tree; it lists each individual page and shows its exact position in the Web site. Customers can use this option to help orient themselves when they become lost.

Check Download Times

You may have a state-of-the-art modem, but recall that most Web surfers are saddled with older or outdated versions. So . . . while your computer may be able to download your site pages in an instant, somebody else might have to wait a lot longer. You want to avoid as much of *everyone's* waiting time as possible, so be willing to experiment. Surf your site using a variety of modem speeds—make sure that most of your pages can be accessed quickly, even with a mediocre 28.8 modem. (Don't worry too much about the real dinosaurs.) If wait times are high, adjust the page to fix the problem. Eliminate graphics, sound, animation, or whatever else might be necessary.

Seek Friendly Advice

While you're in the testing stage, enlist friends and family to help you out. They usually make reliable yet cheap labor! Assign them various shopping "tasks" or goals, and have them try to navigate your site in pursuit of a product or information. Then be willing to accept criticism! Ask them questions along these lines:

1. How can we better organize the site?
2. What, if anything, confused you?
3. What, if anything, annoyed you?
4. Was it easy to find all the information you needed?
5. How can we improve the shopping experience?

Once you have done what you can with inside advice, solicit the opinions of those not connected to you or the company. Even after you debut the online store, you can continue to use customer feedback to improve your site. Offer a brief, voluntary survey about the site organization, appearance, and contents. Naturally, not many visitors will be willing to take the time without receiving something in return—humans are a mercenary lot! To encourage feedback, offer a small bonus like free shipping, a discount, or a complimentary sample. Once you begin receiving advice, make sure you actually pay attention. Don't just stick the data in a stack of papers and forget about it—otherwise the whole process was a waste of time.

Online Purchasing

An Overview

The online shopping section at this time is probably the most important part of a Web site. These screens help streamline and support the fact-finding process, which often leads to the actual purchase of your goods or services. Even if customers cannot actually buy anything directly from your store, the information you provide will promote offline sales—either in the bricks-and-mortar store or by phone, fax, or e-mail. Thus, the shopping content plays a central role in e-commerce;

all stores should try to build at least a simple site to represent their interests on the Internet.

Yet if your company is capable of more, you'll want to seriously consider supporting an online purchasing zone. Purchasing was discussed briefly in Chapter 2—it's a secure online site where transactions can actually take place in cyberspace. Despite the heightened trouble and risk involved in online purchasing, one undeniable fact remains: It's the future of commerce. Businesses that get a head start by developing their secure sites now will have a much easier road in the years to come. If you *are* considering the possibility, there are many elements beyond the secure server that you'll have to integrate. Online purchasing is entirely different from the shopping application—it even takes place on a separate server. Still, it follows a fairly standard pattern of action.

- **Initiation.** The customer commences the purchasing process by deciding to buy a particular product. While viewing a catalog page, he clicks on the proper button or link: "Buy this item," or perhaps simply "Purchase." The customer is then transferred from the shopping site to the online purchasing site. At this point, the customer is interacting with a secure server. All the information he provides will be encrypted and protected from hackers. Aside from personal preferences or brief surveys, never ask for private information before the customer is protected by the proper measures.

- **Order Confirmation.** The first screen a customer normally sees is a summary of product(s) he has chosen. Now he is free to adjust the order to his own specifications—depending on the product, he might change order quantity, choose a color or size, personalize the item, or fine-tune any number of other characteristics. The customer should also still have the option to change his mind. There should be a "Back" or "Cancel purchase" button built into the application. If selected, the links would transfer the shopper back to the last catalog page he had viewed. Otherwise, once satisfied with the current order, the customer can choose "Accept."

- **Customer Information.** Now that the customer has confirmed his intent to buy merchandise, he should feel comfortable entering personal data. This page should essentially be a form, with fields for entering the desired shipping address and the customer's contact information (if different). As desired, your company can also provide options such as gift-wrapping, either free or for a charge, rush shipping, etc. On this page, there should be additional material informing the customer of the expected shipping date and time until delivery. Always overestimate. It is better for customers to be pleasantly surprised than for them to wait two weeks for an item that was supposed to arrive in three or four days. Lastly, you'll need to request payment information; customers will usually choose to pay with a credit card. If for some reason the customer wishes to use a check, then skip the following payment verification step. Once all of this data has been entered, the customer should see a total price, including any tax, and then finalize the end of the transaction by clicking "Accept" or perhaps "Send order."

- **Payment Verification.** At this point, the customer often waits while the server verifies the payment data with your chosen institution. It usually takes less than thirty seconds. During this time, the customer should see some sort of indication that your company is processing the order—as well as an estimate as to how long the step will take. This way, there's no dead time during which the customer wonders if something went wrong.

- **Confirmation Screen.** Once the payment has been approved, the customer is finally shuttled to a confirmation screen, which concludes the purchasing process. This page should thank the customer—by name, if possible—and confirm that the order should be arriving within the specified amount of time. You might even provide a final list of the items that were ordered, so that the customer is reassured that he will be receiving the correct merchandise. The customer should then have the option of returning to the shopping site—perhaps a "Back to the main menu" button. Around this time, the actual transfer of funds will take place between the customer's account and your business's merchant account. Now it's up to you to deliver a quality product on time!

- **Batch Transfer.** After the customer has completed a purchase, the order will be stored on the Web server until the next transfer takes place. The term *batch transaction* is used to describe the process whereby your online system transfers the most recent batch of orders to your internal computer system. At this point, the orders will be officially recognized by your business, and you can begin to fulfill them and then ship the merchandise. You can also update your product inventories. Batch transactions occur at predetermined times, according to your own needs. Smaller companies are usually satisfied with either one or two transfers per day—larger corporations may arrange for one every few minutes!

Accepting Credit Cards

Credit cards are deservedly the most popular Internet payment option. First, they're extremely convenient for customers, who don't have to do any extra footwork to arrange the disbursement. All they need is one valid existing card. After filling out a brief form, they can often expect the order within a few days.

Merchants, too, find them easy to work with, since the transactions are generally completed within forty-eight hours. During the actual purchase, the payments are immediate, since nothing needs to be exchanged through the mail system. There's also no lengthy waiting period *after* the order, as there is with traditional checks. Customer credit accounts can even be validated while they wait; with this option, the transaction is not confirmed until the payment has been processed. The delay is negligible, and it allows both merchant and customer to proceed in the confidence that no payment problems will arise. If you have online purchasing, you *definitely* need to accept credit cards; the general list includes Visa, American Express, MasterCard, Discover, and sometimes even Diner's Club. You can arrange the details with your own acquirer once you obtain an Internet merchant account. Your ISP or turnkey can usually handle the actual transaction.

You may still accept checks or money orders in exchange for goods and services, but such a form of payment cannot be verified online. They work best for companies without online purchasing, or as an alternative for those customers who will not or cannot use a credit card. Be aware that such traditional, mail-order techniques will entail traditional shipping delays. Customers would not receive their purchase for at least a couple of weeks.

Handling Fraud

If your company accepts credit cards—and it almost certainly will—then at some point you're going to have to deal with credit card fraud. People will try to use stolen cards to make purchases, or customers will buy something and then deny that they ever received it. In a bricks-and-mortar store, it's easy to ask customers for a picture ID to verify identity, then use their signatures on the receipts as proof if they later contest the charge. Naturally, on the Web it's impossible to do either one of these things—and criminals know this. That's why you have to use every technique in your power to prevent fraudulent charges.

- **The Address Verification System.** The address verification system, commonly known as AVS, is a key component in fraud prevention. Most banks offer this service to customers with a merchant account, so be sure to take advantage of it. The AVS checks the address and shipping information that the customer provides with its own database—and it notifies you if it finds any inconsistencies. In theory, the credit card user should be having the product shipped to the cardholder's address, that is, to her own home. There are some exceptions, of course. Criminals sometimes take advantage of the gift option available at many stores, in which the customer can have the item sent directly to someone else. They will then enter their own PO box or address and charge the purchase to the unwitting victim. You help prevent such tactics by requiring the customer to enter her own address along with the recipient's. Exceptions to the address rule may occur if the customer has recently moved. In that case, ask her to fax in proof of address along with a valid ID. We know that this sounds a bit harsh, but it can save your company a great deal of trouble down the road.

- **Signed Receipts.** Even though the customers may not be able to sign a receipt at the point of purchase, at least they can sign one upon delivery. *Always* require a signature for all of your company's deliveries, and then make sure that you keep hard copies of these receipts on file. They can be your only defense if a customer claims that the product never arrived.

Hopefully, AVS will protect you from most incidences of fraud. But no matter how careful your company is, you'll eventually have to deal with the specter of charge backs. Charge backs occur when a customer successfully disputes the charges incurred on his card. They are allowed to file the paperwork with their credit card company within a certain number of days after receiving their bill. After you have been notified, you then have thirty days to contest the charge back. You're supposed to prove that the purchase was, indeed, valid and that it was placed by the cardholder. If they passed the AVS check, you can try to use that—or you can always look for that delivery receipt you so wisely preserved. Other than that, however, your chances aren't so great. That's why you should be as careful as you can *before* the purchase is processed.

Why is the prevention of charge backs so important? First of all, they're time-consuming and inconvenient. You want your employees to spend time encouraging new transactions, not fixing old ones. Charge backs also play havoc with your accounting system, for obvious reasons. But most of all, an excess of charge backs will ruin your credit reputation. If your acquirer decides that your business is risky, it can drop you—and that is very, very bad. So be vigilant. Keep your charge backs to an absolute minimum.

Online Purchasing Tips

Shopping Carts

Normally, when a shopper is ready to make a purchase on the Internet, he selects an item by clicking on its purchase button. The transaction moves to the secure server, the customer fills out his information, and then he submits the order. This process works extremely well when the shopper is only buying one item—but what about shoppers who are looking to buy three, four, five, or more items at one particular store? With traditional software, the customers would be required to fill out that same order form multiple times, and after each transaction they'd be routed back to the shopping area and forced to start over. *Anyone* would be irritated by such repetition. It's a total waste of everyone's time—even merchants hate having to receive several separate order forms for the same person.

Fortunately, there's an alternative: Internet shopping carts. If you've ever browsed in a large online store, you're probably familiar with this application. The software, which you can purchase off-the-shelf, remembers customers' multiple orders at a single session, so they can buy everything in one fell swoop. This both reduces the customer frustration level and helps a merchant keep orders organized.

Shopping carts both streamline your ordering process and please your customers!

When you load the application, a shopping cart icon will appear in a designated location on each of your catalog pages. If a customer decides to purchase a particular item, she can click on the "Add to shopping cart" button, which will then shift her to a new page that lists everything in her particular cart. It will also post the per-item price and allow the shopper to adjust the desired quantity. After viewing the results, the customer can click one more button to return to the main shopping site. During this process, the merchant server places a temporary cookie file on the customer's computer—the file will store all information about this particular session. Each time the customer adds something else to her shopping cart, the cookie records the item, adding it to the growing list. As the customer shops, she is free to add or delete items as she chooses; the cookie will remember everything necessary unless the customer logs off of the site—then it's back to a clean slate. When shoppers are ready, they can head to "checkout," that is, your online purchasing area, in order to finish the transaction. They can choose to buy everything in their shopping cart at once, thus avoiding the need to repeat the same action several times. At this point, the temporary cookie is deleted.

Shopping cart software is fairly cheap and easy to install. Your company should definitely invest in the technology if it stocks more than a dozen or so products. Because the carts are so popular with large stores right now, they lend your own site an air of legitimacy. Besides, it's always wise to do what you can to make the shopping experience as pleasant as possible. Most surfers love shopping carts—and even if they don't, they aren't forced to use this option. So, using this application is a pretty safe action. The exception is if your company only sells a few different things. It's silly to have a shopping cart when your whole catalog can sit above the fold on a single page! In these cases, it's best to have shoppers fill out an order form with check boxes for item type and quantity. With a single order form, they'll still be able to complete the purchase in one trip.

Consider Alternative E-Payments

Unfortunately, credit cards are not perfect. As useful as they are, even credit cards have drawbacks. For one thing, not all customers have one. Some customers' credit history is too poor, a few people have just never gotten around to applying for one (it's true!), and others don't feel secure using anything but cash or checks. In addition, even a lot of people who *do* own cards prefer to reserve them for emergencies only. If you compel your customers to pay online with a credit card, you might be losing out on sales. (Checks are still an option, but they take a relatively long time to receive and process.) Another problem is bank-imposed per-transaction charges. If you sell smaller items, such as fridge magnets or auto parts, the added fee takes a huge bite out of the profit. Nobody wants to lose half of a $10 sale!

Thankfully, necessity is still the mother of invention. Almost before the problems began, entrepreneurs began working to find alternatives to credit cards. They have been quite successful; by now, dozens of resourceful companies have generated alternative methods of online payment. No method is perfect, but each has its own advantages. Listed below are a few of the more common options.

• **Electronic Cash.** Electronic cash is currently enjoying a surge in popularity, since it combines the ease of normal cash payments with virtual transactions. So how is this possible? Third-party companies—notably CyberCash, Mercantile Bank, and Digi-Cash—agree to act as the middlemen between merchants and customers. Customers purchase a product online, but they pay for it with a special account maintained by an e-cash provider. The store can then receive instant payment into their own account at the same service provider. Given these parameters, electronic cash not surprisingly necessitates footwork by both parties: An Internet customer must open an account with one of these "service bureaus," then deposit a certain amount of money. In turn, the merchant must also have an account with the e-cash providers. During the actual transaction, then, the money simply jumps from one internal account to another. Granted, this process is a bit unwieldy. After all, the customer and merchant must go to a lot of trouble in advance to permit the sale. So why does anyone bother with e-cash?

There's two main reasons. The most important one is simply that many online shoppers still feel uncomfortable about transmitting their personal data over the Internet. E-cash is then an attractive option, because customers can set up their account over the phone. They only have to give their information out one time, instead of during each and every sale. This reduces the chance that a hacker will eventually commandeer credit card numbers or even a customer identity. People also feel more secure giving actual people their data; it's more comfortable than filling in a generic, public-looking form.

The other reason that e-cash is so popular is that it can be used for micropayments. Any flat fee levied by banks in most credit card transactions is prohibitively high for minor purchases. If you sell an item for $3, by the time you're finished paying for the transaction fees you've almost *lost* money! In these cases, credit cards just aren't worth the trouble or expense. E-cash, however, allows for the disbursement of smaller amounts of money. CyberCash has led the way in this instance, with its introduction of CyberCoins. Customers in the Cyber-Coin program are allowed to withdraw money from their offline account and deposit it into an electronic wallet. They can then make withdrawals from their "wallet" for any amount of money up to the total balance—even so-called micropayments of a few cents or a couple dollars. Unlike credit card companies, Cyber-Cash charges fees appropriate to small purchases.

The convenience of electronic cash is debatable. During the transaction, it's about as quick as using a credit card. Yet the middleman provider is also allowed to withhold payment from the merchant for various periods of time—even up to a couple of months—depending on a variety of factors. The customer, too, is put through the onetime rigmarole of setting up the account.

Yet beyond these irritations, the biggest problem with electronic cash is that the system is useless unless customers subscribe to it as well. It's kind of like buying a videophone—the possibilities are great, but they're still too new to be truly useful. Who wants to buy a videophone if you don't know anybody else who has one? Yet even now, many customers are still willing to join because of concerns about online security. The number of habitual online shoppers also continues to rise steeply, and perhaps soon electronic cash will be as ordinary as an ATM. In that event, you'll definitely want to consider acquiring an e-cash account.

- **Demand Drafts.** These are another great option for those customers who prefer paying with checks yet dislike the long wait necessary for processing. Demand drafts are just like regular checks, except the customers don't have to fill them out and mail them in. Instead, they call a third-party bureau and provide their financial information over the phone: bank, account number, phone number, etc. The service company then prints a check that looks very similar to a normal personal check, only—

of course—without the signature. It then deposits the payment, and the funds are directed to your company, minus the company's own transaction fee.

Demand drafts are extremely useful to merchants; they cut down on the lengthy waits involved when customers mail in a personal check. You will have to pay hundreds of dollars in set-up costs for the service, but the processing fees are usually less than those charged by credit card companies. Because the drafts can be processed on a repeat basis, they are ideal for recurring payments, such as loans or other such bills. Not only can customers pay online, but they can set up the automatic payment of a recurring bill. Such a system is beneficial to both parties. Just be careful that you observe the strict regulations associated with demand drafts. Since they involve payment without the physical presence or signature of the customer, the business community must be very careful not to be accused of fraud. Talk to your legal consultant for further advice about demand drafts.

- **Electronic Checks.** Electronic checks are a brand new form of e-payment, almost like state-of-the-art demand drafts. A customer registers with a merchant by providing the company with all of her pertinent banking information. This information is then stored with the merchant and used in all future transactions. Because e-checks—like demand drafts—entail repeat business, they are now almost exclusively used for recurring bills. A customer can check her bill online, perhaps using a special password to gain access to her account with the merchant, and then merely okay the payment without having to reenter her private data every time. If they so desire, customers can usually also receive their bill via e-mail or snail mail. Because this option is paper-free and fast, it's a safe bet that entrepreneurs will soon be adapting such e-checks for common use in other situations. Amazon uses a similar system with their one-click purchasing option, wherein the store can charge repeat customers with stored information. Shoppers can actually buy items with one click of the mouse! The only difference is that the Amazon system is based on credit cards; it will be interesting to see if e-checks, with a basis in actual bank accounts, will ever rival or overtake the current preference for credit card purchases.

Send Order Confirmations

The ordering process doesn't necessarily end at the checkout.

Many novice online shoppers are a bit unnerved by the simplicity of the process. They fill out a little form, click a button, see a quick "thank you" screen, and are returned to the main menu. How do they know that you even received the order? Did it "work"? How can they be sure that you won't take the money and run? You can quiet these concerns by sending a confirmation notice of every order you receive. Since they're online in the first place, you can almost always provide the notice via a brief e-mail. (Just remember to ask for an address during the order process!) In the note, you would include a list of the goods ordered, including quantity and any other special qualities (color, size, etc.), an estimated shipping time, and another "thank you" for their visit. You can also encourage them to come back soon. E-mail confirmations can be standardized and automated—then your order-processing staff wouldn't even need to worry about remembering to send them. For those few customers without e-mail, you can have them check a special box to request a snail-mail version.

Warranties

Online buyer's remorse can be particularly strong. Many shoppers are initially seduced by low prices and fast shipping; unfortunately, they become anxious later on, as they realize that they just bought something sight unseen. Then the dreaded word "return" rears its ugly head. Your goal, not surprisingly, is to minimize the panic and keep customers happy even after they buy a product. To some extent, their regret can be mitigated by a good shopping experience. If your store has a good online front, if you post testimonials, provide pictures, and otherwise assure the customer that she hasn't made a huge mistake, then customers are less likely to change their minds after the fact.

Still, many people could use a little something extra to tip them from undecided to regular client, and one thing you can do is offer warranties. The details would depend entirely on your company and products, but the key is that shoppers should be aware that the quality of the product is in some way assured. Services, too, can carry a warranty; if you repair appliances, you can certify your work for a three-year period. Customers would be able to view the warranty before they move to the secure server; then, after they have purchased the product, you should mail them a copy for their records. Do anything you must in order to keep customers from returning items.

Clearly Advertise Your Security Measures

Make the effort to reassure customers that your business is both legitimate and secure.

Customers worried about entering their private information might be mollified if you post your security measures in an obvious place. It's a good idea to place such information at the top of the page where customers are required to enter their name, address, credit card information, etc. The process is not as intimidating if they have just read a summary of your encryption devices and customer protection policies. Even if this particular page is too cluttered to post your assurances in their entirety, at least provide a link to them—perhaps "Click here for information about our customer security policies."

Offer Money-Back Guarantees

If returns are so very troublesome to merchants, then why should you offer customers a money-back guarantee? Experienced managers know the answer to this one: because a lot of people will not buy things if they don't have the option to return them. Customers can be extremely skittish, especially when they shop online. If they feel like they don't have a safety net, they're not as likely to spend their money in the first place. In real life, people usually feel more confident about their ability to detect quality items—and they're usually right. And yet bricks-and-mortar companies often *still* maintain a return policy. Just imagine, then, how important it is in cyberspace. Online, customers need merchants to stake their livelihood on the quality of their products. You won't be forced into anything, but pure competition might change your mind: If you won't countenance a return policy, then someone else will. Feel free, however, to stipulate a few conditions. Set a deadline after which the guarantee is no longer valid. Thirty days is usually perceived as a reasonable amount of time. Also, require the customer to show proof of purchase—usually the receipt—in order to protect yourself from fraudulent claims.

If you do provide a guarantee, make sure you don't forget to advertise it. Mention it frequently on your shopping site, and maintain a special page that outlines the policy in detail. If customers don't know about the guarantee in advance, it won't do your sales any good. The idea is to seduce shoppers who are still undecided, not please customers who already bought something!

Always Offer Free Information

The Internet is a great leveling force in that it creates stiff competition between various companies that want to survive. As businesses work frantically to adapt to the brutal pace, customers have become more powerful than ever. Since customers have the ability to choose from hundreds of options at the click of a mouse, companies have discovered that in order to maintain loyalty, they must give something extra, a little bit more than whatever the guy down the street is offering. This is largely why so many Internet start-up companies have been failing—in their rush to attract customers, they have forgotten how to make money!

Knowing this information, unfortunately, does not make you any more able to avoid reality. Undeniable customer power means that online companies walk a very, very thin line between competitiveness and profitability. To this effect, your company needs to be careful about how it works to generate cash, so as not to annoy frugal customers.

It's definitely okay to charge for your own products and offline services, since they constitute your livelihood. No customer will be expecting you to give away free merchandise on a regular basis! Other things, however, should be granted to the customers without charging a single dime: Information is one prime example.

Although in real life newspapers and magazines can charge a flat fee for their informational services, such online information should be given away for free. Why? Because if you don't, then some other Web site will—and customers will flock to the site with the best deal. This is where it comes down to your willingness to cannibalize your own profits and customer base. If you accept such occurrences as necessary to survival, then you'll probably be fine. When you become known as a source of quality information, surfers will visit your site and spend their money in other ways. On the flip side, if you absolutely refuse to allow open access, then you'd better pack it in right now. Intellectual property is a lot looser concept on the Internet!

Test Ship in Advance

Although online purchasing is extremely easy for the customer, the merchant's task isn't nearly so simple. Behind the scenes, the store must coordinate a wide variety of tasks, all of which must work smoothly together in order to deliver the customer's correct order on time. If anything is missing or faulty in some way, your entire venture can be a disaster. You need to work out the kinks *before* your Internet store opens, and in order to do that you must run plenty of test ships.

Enlist several coworkers, friends or family members to help you out. (Perhaps the ones who helped you debug your shopping site.) Ask them to "buy" a variety of items online—in different combinations, quantities, etc.—and to have the products shipped to locations at the extremities of your business sphere. At this point, some advice about the purchasing process is always welcome, but you'll probably be more concerned with simply seeing if the system functions! Go through this process as many times as your company needs to ensure an efficient, accurate order fulfillment and shipping process. It is *far* better to delay the opening date than to screw up a large number of initial orders.

Our shipping philosophy: Practice, practice, practice!

Allow Customers an "Out"

Never corner potential customers by forcing them to use online purchasing.

Even if you have done everything in your power to make customers comfortable with the online order process, you should still offer them an escape route. After all, nothing is foolproof. Once they have entered your secure server, some customers might change their minds at the last minute and leave the entire site. Perhaps they are just still too uncomfortable about sharing their private information. If a more skittish shopper goes to the order site and finds that he *must* either enter a credit card number or other account information, he might flee the scene!

You can help prevent the loss of potential customers by posting other means of payment on your online shopping pages. Include the option to print out an order form, so that the customer can mail it in with a check or money order. Also, make sure you include your 800 order number on every page. These alternatives remind the customer that she is not being forced to breach her privacy; it also helps reassure the customer that yours is a legitimate business.

Getting Your Site up and Running

Once you have finished designing the Web site, you'll need to actually move the files from the computer hard drive onto the server. The process involves the use of "File Transfer Protocol," and is thus informally known as ftp-ing. It is also often referred to as "uploading," since it's the exact opposite of downloading—instead of pulling data, you're sending it. Ftp-ing requires the use of special software, much of which can be acquired for free online. If you don't already have a company homepage, you'll need to obtain the appropriate computer applications either from the relevant Internet sites or a local store. Your basic HTML files will be sent first, usually starting with a file marked INDEX.HTML, then followed by all of the little extras you may have chosen to include: graphics, sound, video, etc. Your server's help line should be able to help you with any thorny technical questions.

Chapter 5

Behind the Scenes

Up until this point, we have mainly discussed how to build and design the public face of an online store. Indeed, it is certainly important to pay close attention to the applications that customers will interact with. Nobody wants to shop in a dimly lit, dingy, poorly stocked store—and yet thousands of companies post disorganized, cluttered Web sites every year. Your image will profoundly affect sales, and sales are what business is all about. Still, no matter how effective your storefront may be, you must have the internal support to back it up.

Without good back-office support, your online venture will fail.

Launching a Web site is like staging an elaborate play. Sure, the script and set are important, but no production on earth can survive backstage mismanagement. Suppose a stagehand were to erect the wrong scenery for the big finale? What if rusted cables break, dropping a sandbag on your lead soprano? Worse yet, what if everyone in the cast personally hates one another? It might make onstage performances a bit tense!

When you manage an online store, then, you must pay careful attention to what goes on behind the scenes. You must ship your merchandise on time, prevent interdepartmental squabbles, and provide for adequate site maintenance. No customer will remember how nice your store looks when her order never arrives. You also want to be on the lookout for any advance or technique that might enhance the success of your company. Overseeing operations is, after all, your primary job!

Facilitate Communication

Good business requires a large number of disparate elements to work in concert. Accounting, shipping, customer support, information technology, and management all play crucial roles in the process. Yet when one department becomes too involved in its own duties, it might begin to ignore or ride roughshod over the needs of other coworkers. You almost certainly already deal with these issues on a regular basis. Nevertheless, creating an online presence will affect *every* department at your store. In Chapter 1, we discussed how vital it is for you to investigate the possible changes before you even make the shift. The task certainly does not end with the store's debut! Opening a new sales arena might very well rock the company boat in unpleasant ways. It's extremely important for you to work hard to prevent conflicts, both during the transition and after your company moves online. Each department should be made to feel like part of a single team, not individuals competing for scarce resources. Coworkers are partners, not competitors.

Emphasize the importance of interdepartmental communication. Encourage everyone to share ideas and suggestions. Sales representatives should be in close contact with the shipping folks, helping them keep tabs on customer concerns and special requests. The accounting department needs to send the salespeople updates on individuals known to engage in credit card fraud, and IT should help the marketing execs keep track of the latest advertising technologies. Most important, everyone needs to be nice to the frequently overstressed IT department. When the site crashes, the techies do *not* appreciate being besieged with angry complaints from other departments. They are already doing their best to remedy the situation, and you will certainly get faster results if coworkers exercise tact. So you get the picture. Frequent communication amongst *all* the departments will help prevent misunderstandings and promote harmony.

Intranets

To this end, you might want to implement a company Intranet—that is, if you don't already have one. Unless your business employs only a few people, Intranets are the most efficient way for coworkers to stay in contact. They are essentially internal Internets, accessible only by employees of a particular company, who also have the correct personal password.

Intranets can host the company databases, statistics, market research, mission statement, special reports, interoffice e-mail, and anything else that might be of value to employees. Having immediate access to such data is a definite boon for workers in an information-driven market. Where communication is easy, it also tends to occur more frequently. Intranets can be an incredibly unifying component of your business. Talk to your IT department to see if you have the necessary resources.

Extranets

Oftentimes a corporate Intranet is not enough. After all, your internal data is extremely useful—to some degree—to people not directly employed by your company. Think about it. Your distributors could benefit from up-to-date inventory and shipping information; your partners could use the latest data on your new products; the turnkey that handles your order processing needs all kinds of information. Even certain subcategories of customers might enjoy a restricted site directed towards their individual needs. Keeping your internal databases guarded is certainly wise, but a certain level of information-sharing is vital to the modern business. That's why Extranets are such a powerful tool.

Extranets are special Intranets; unlike internal networks, they're created for interests outside the physical boundaries of your company. They generally have unpublished URLs, since they are not for the general public. Extranets are also usually password-protected, as a safeguard for your business's sensitive information. One business could conceivably support several Extranet sites simultaneously, depending on its ability to sustain each network.

....

Encourage the free exchange of information.
Knowledge is power!

....

If you run a company that designs and sells furniture, you might create one Extranet solely for your suppliers. It could permit access to your current inventory, or perhaps describe new products, so your suppliers can predict when you'll need a new shipment of various tools or raw materials. They can then stock appropriate amounts of supplies before you even need to request a new shipment. Your partners might desire information on market research or product specifications, pricing, and availability, so they can make well-informed decisions without having to call repeatedly and waste your own valuable time. Extranets make it easier for them to tailor their customer advertisements to your output. Even your regular customers might enjoy a site that offers them special discounts, or sneak peeks at upcoming designs. In essence, Extranets are valuable to almost anyone who has a valid stake in your company.

Tracking Online Availability

Customers who shop online expect the most efficient service possible. No customer wants to purchase an item only to be notified two days later that the store is out of stock, and that the order won't actually arrive for a few weeks. In a bricks-and-mortar store, this doesn't really happen. The merchandise is either on the floor, in the stockroom, or not available.

On the Web, the problem is much more serious. In an already hectic business environment, it can be exceedingly difficult to reconcile a fluctuating inventory with unpredictable customer demand. If you currently have only ten of one particular lamp, you must carefully monitor the exact number of items that are sold. It's all too easy to sell out, and then have three or four more people "purchase" the lamp before you can pull the option off of the site. You are now in a rather sticky situation—several people are waiting expectantly for a nonexistent product to arrive within a business week. You have two options: You can scramble to have the product rush-delivered from a different supplier, or you can send an apologetic note explaining either the delay or the cancellation, depending on the situation. Both choices are unattractive.

Even if you manage to locate and rush-ship the item, you're still paying an exorbitant price for the opportunity—and the charge *will* be pretty ugly. On the other hand, if you opt for the note indicating either a shipping delay or complete unavailability, you risk losing customers. No shopper wants to go through the hassle of obtaining an online refund more than once, and they very likely won't visit your store again. When you earn a reputation for being unreliable, your online venture will suffer.

So what to do? Even if you sell only a few kinds of products, updating the Web site inventory can be a full-time job. Companies that sell a wide variety of merchandise may find the task impossible. Smaller businesses can often post a simple notice that "Stock is limited" or that the item is "Subject to availability." Such disclaimers can help warn shoppers in advance. This avenue works best with companies that do not provide online purchasing; in that case, make sure that your sales representatives have access to an internal database. Your company's Intranet or database can keep an accurate inventory record, so that when the customer calls in or e-mails the order, the employee would immediately know if the items are sold out. At that point, the sales representative can warn the caller that the order may take a few weeks. The shopper might be a bit irritated, but at least she didn't complete the sale.

This is exactly why online purchasing poses a slight risk. Unless great care is taken to ensure that catalog availability is current, customers might proceed through the entire process, including payment, before being notified later that the order cannot be filled. As mentioned previously, online orders are often transferred to the internal systems in batches, at set times during the day. But the batch system does not provide instant feedback. If, at the beginning of the day, you have six model cars on hand, then the Web site will assume that they are available until told otherwise. Suppose, then, that eight orders show up in the next daily batch. Uh oh.

....
Never be too optimistic when posting shipping times;
you'll be setting yourself up to fail.
....

There are two ways to prevent such problems. One is to simply be incredibly conservative when posting estimated shipping times. If you have only ten of one item on hand, post a message such as "Please allow up to three weeks for delivery." This way, even if you run out of merchandise, at least you can try to produce some more before the time limit expires. Of course, the drawback is that customers might decline to purchase your product because of the expected delay, when it is probable that you would be able to ship it within a few days! Do some market research to determine how your existing customers view the importance of fast delivery. If most of them seem willing to wait, then this is probably the safest and cheapest option. If your target market prizes a fast response, however, then you should consider developing a real-time inventory.

Real-Time Inventories

If your business has both impatient customers *and* the necessary resources, you can link the Web server to your internal inventory database. If these two systems were able to communicate with one another, you would be able to provide your customers with accurate, immediate information about their orders. When the Web site has access to your inventory, it knows instantly whether or not the product is available. This allows customers to view up-to-date shipping estimates. If the product is currently on hand, the site will post a message that the item will ship within a few days; if it has recently sold out, the product message will instead inform the shopper that a wait should be expected. The integration of your internal and external services is expensive and time-consuming, but if you are capable of handling the task, it can really give your business the edge in customer service.

If you are in this situation, you definitely need to consider using XML to program your online site. Remember that XML allows for a relatively simple interface between incompatible systems, so it could save you a great deal of time, money and frustration. In addition, it lets you modify the content in new ways once it is brought to the Web site. If your internal system tracks merchandise by serial number, you won't necessarily want that to be listed prominently at the store—after all, the numbers are meaningless to customers. Yet if you simply import the data from your database, it would be posted in the same format, serial numbers and all. Luckily, certain XML programs allow you to both import *and* manipulate the format of incoming data, so that you can customize your Web site without a great deal of fuss.

Whether or not you decide to base your venture on XML, talk to your IT people to see what software and how much money might be required for your business to link the Internet with your internal systems. It's a big decision either way, so do not attempt this process until you have carefully weighed the costs involved.

• **Firewalls.** If you decide to link your personal, real-time inventory with your Web site, you'll want to implement a number of safety precautions. After all, if your internal databases are joined with the public area of the store, your company's most sensitive information may be at risk. The constant flow of information between the two systems is particularly defenseless; it's like an open castle gate, a vulnerable point at which intruders will likely try to break in. And, if an unauthorized party infiltrates your system at this point, he can do extensive damage to your business.

  The best defense is to erect barriers called firewalls. They monitor and restrict access to your internal computer system, making it much more difficult for hackers to breach security. The simplest, most common type of firewall is generated by a "bastion host." A bastion host is a special computer that maintains connections to both your internal network and the Internet. It restricts traffic between these networks through the use of a "proxy server," which carefully screens the flow of information. Only authorized requests for information are allowed to pass through. In this way, a proxy server is a lot like an electronic sentry. Other firewalls will monitor the origin and destination of each transmission and reroute any that are unauthorized.

There are currently many different ways to protect your business from outside tampering. Just keep in mind that firewalls are not optional! If you plan to integrate your internal and external operations, you must implement appropriate security measures. Talk to your ISP or your IT department to see what types of barriers will work best for your company.

Handling Returns

If you want customers to buy things from your online store, you'll almost certainly need to have a return policy. To a great extent, this will be similar to the policy your store already has. Any stipulations of product quality, in fact, can be the same as you would normally expect. The fact the customer bought a CD over the Internet does not mean that he can return it in any condition; feel free to deny a return if the CD has already been opened.

The only policy differences, really, have to do with timing and payment. If you already run a mail-order operation, then you've probably already established reasonable parameters. If not, then you should make some adjustments. It's easy to set a time limit on returns when the customer buys something in person, because they take possession of the product on the date of purchase. Online, however, the customer makes the payment days before actually receiving it, so your current policy may be a bit too strict for Internet use. Start the clock from the date you actually *ship* the product, not from the purchase date; that way, customers won't be penalized for a delayed shipment. Shipping data is also easy for you to track; there's no ambiguity. Many companies feel that about ten to fifteen days is long enough for the customers to decide whether they want the item, although that may vary in special circumstances or with certain products. Once you've settled on an acceptable window of time, just add the expected shipping time. If you calculate that almost all packages will arrive in five days or less, you can ask that customers request a return within fifteen days. If your shipments normally take longer, just add a few extra days. Round up to nice numbers—an eighteen-day return policy would raise eyebrows!

Once you've established a time frame, you need to arrange for the actual refund process. Since your customers will probably be paying by credit card, this means you'll need to arrange a refund process with your acquirer. The method by which you can effect a refund will vary from bank to bank, so be sure to check in advance to see what kind of policy yours has. Never give refunds in cash when the purchase has been made by credit card, and always refund the money to the same card number that you have on file—this will help prevent fraud, and it will keep your records neater.

Put Your Knowledge to Use

Smart managers will view their company Web site as a perpetual work in progress. No online store should ever be seen as "finished" because there is always room for adaptation and improvement. Just look around—there are millions of published words of advice on how to fine-tune your Internet page, including this book! Yet despite the abundance of professional ramblings, the most important words are not those that come from the so-called experts. They're the ones that come from your customers.

Internet Web sites are a mother lode of information about your target audience, which is probably why we call the process of analyzing it "data mining." Every time a visitor accesses your store, he leaves all sorts of fingerprints. With the correct software, you can find out any number of things about the profile and shopping habits of your customers. Never waste this opportunity! When armed with customer knowledge, you can tailor your Web site even more perfectly to the needs and wants of your market—and that means increased revenues!

In order to get the best mileage out of your Internet traffic, it's a good idea to maintain one or more sophisticated databases and perhaps even hire an outside analyst to crunch the numbers. Make sure you keep track of every available detail for each and every transaction, and pay close attention to the information you gather in online questionnaires.

Before you start actually gathering the data, ask your experts about which extraction tools they use; extraction tools are programs that interface with a database to highlight and categorize certain parameters. You need only select the pertinent bits of data, and the software does the slave work. For instance: You could run a search on all customers under eighteen who visited more than once last week, or just as easily compile a list of all female visitors who have purchased more than $100 worth of merchandise. This type of search, which seeks concrete results, is the most accepted form of data mining.

Yet there are other types of software that try to reach even further; some packages can be used in an effort to predict the future! They use complex mathematical models and sensitive software to make "intelligent" guesses about future trends for your company. These latter programs are obviously not completely reliable, but they still do a better job of prognostication than do humans. If you use the data wisely, in fact, the predictions can be surprisingly accurate.

Which type of extraction tools you use is entirely up to you. But regardless of your choice, you still need to investigate yet another quality: compatibility. The efficiency of your data mining depends on the compatibility of your extraction tools with each database. Linking the tools with more than one database can be difficult if they are based on different protocols. Therefore, to minimize hassle, they should be "ODBC compliant." ODBC, or Open Database Connectivity, refers to a certain set of standard protocols that have been created to allow programmers to build interfaces with databases more quickly; they no longer have to start from scratch each time. The benefit of having ODBC compliance for your software parallels the standardization of car parts—rather than having to find or create special replacements for every single make or model, mass production has allowed parts to be interchanged and used in a large number of models. In other words, an extraction tool needs to connect in some solid way with the database that it's "mining"; ODBC standards just make it easier for software developers to build that very connection.

Once the necessary interfaces have been established, it's time to sit back and start interpreting that huge tangle of data. This can be time consuming but rewarding; the beauty of data mining exists in the ability of people to distill valuable information from chaos. In order to obtain the best results, you'll especially want to keep track of the following categories.

Demographics

Tracking the demographics of your clientele is relatively easy. You can provide a brief, voluntary survey for customers to fill out while visiting your site. As mentioned in Chapter 3, a small giveaway is usually enough to encourage a high return rate. It's usually best to design such a form with simple radio buttons and check boxes, so customers can complete it in less than a minute. Inquire about gender, age range, ethnicity, and/or a general area of residence. You can even discover more personal information: your customers' marital status, number of children, or range of household income. Keep the questions neutral and businesslike. Assure customers that the information will not be sold and will be used only for private purposes.

Always allow visitors to remain anonymous, or your response rate will drop dramatically.

The demographic data that you gather from questionnaires is best used to accomplish two objectives:

....

The first rule of sales: Know thy clientele!

....

1. *You can better design your Web site to accommodate your actual market.* Before you go online, you'll probably have a pretty good idea about what demographics your product will best attract. After all, your existing customers themselves are a solid indication of your largest customer base. You also probably spent some time doing the market research to supplement this data. Nevertheless, no amount of expert predictions, consultant wizardry, or other business voodoo can come close to the accuracy of real-world experience! The customer base you build on the Web may very well differ greatly from those you cater to at your bricks-and-mortar business.

    Think about it. Perhaps your rural real-life business sells homemade jams and jellies to older, more traditional customers. Once launched on the Web, however, that core clientele may suddenly drown in an avalanche of computer-savvy, young, and trendy consumers who love organic products. Nobody can predict this kind of outcome with any level of certainty; the only way to find out is to keep track of actual Web traffic. And, obviously, doing such research is highly important—no sane company would present to an older demographic the same image as they would to young environmental activists!

2. *You can attract advertisements.* Companies are a lot more willing to pay for ads or sponsor various business activities if you can prove that you attract an audience similar to *their* core clientele. This will be discussed more in depth in Chapter 6.

Transaction Trends

Keeping an eye on customer purchasing habits will help you maintain good inventory levels; you can phase out unpopular items, while stocking up on those that are flying off your virtual shelves. But that's Data Management 101—it works only on a mass analysis level. Current software programs are far more discriminating. They can help you cross-analyze customer transactions using thousands of different search queries:

- What percentage of customers buy both nails and hammers, as opposed to only one of the two?

- Are people who live in rural areas less likely to want scented candles?

- What products are first-time customers most inclined to purchase?

- How does that compare to your frequent shoppers?

- Which advertised products experienced the greatest surge in sales?

This information has incalculable value to any online business. First, it will revolutionize your suggestive sales technique. As any manager knows, tracking customer habits will often highlight items that they would be most likely to buy. A shopper that always aims for deli meats might respond well to advertised sales on bologna or cuts of roast beef. Of course, such ads would have no effect on the vegetarians—but that's the beauty of the Internet. A site is capable of being personalized to the degree that coupons can appear for an audience of one. You can actually offer discounts to a single person, based specifically on his past purchase habits. All you need are electronic cookies. To make it easier, you can even have customers log on as "members" of your store; then each customer would view a site tailored to her own unique interests.

Granted, many grocery stores are accomplishing a similar task. In certain big-chain stores, personal coupons are created for each customer at checkout. The store's computer analyzes the data from your scanned-in purchases, then prints coupons for related items. If you buy puppy chow, the discount might be for one dollar off of a box of dog biscuits. It's a brilliant suggestive sales technique. Yet the Internet versions are still better. Personalized bricks-and-mortar coupons can only be printed after the fact—you can't pick them up as you walk in the door. Yet an online store can do exactly that: As soon as the server reads and analyzes your computer's cookie, it can post ads for items you'll want even as the first page loads. There's no way to lose the coupon or forget about the discount. Now *that's* service! (And profit!)

In addition to revamping your suggestive sales, transaction analysis can also help you modify stock, speed the shopping process, and ultimately both increase your profits and please customers. If you don't currently have such software, seriously consider making the investment for your Internet store. Also be willing to hire an expert to interpret the results.

Click Trails

Demographics help you adjust the focus of your Web site, and transaction analysis helps you personalize your ads. Both are excellent tools for online stores, and yet both are also available—to some extent—in bricks-and-mortar businesses. The study of click trails, however, is entirely the property of virtual storefronts. So what exactly are they?

Although relatively new, click trails are very effective; don't hesitate to use them!

"Click trail" is the term used to describe the exact progress of a single customer through your Web site. From the time your first page loads, any visitor will move from page to page in a certain order, each time with the option to click on any available link. Certain online programs can track the unique click trail of each visitor that loads your homepage, whether or not they wind up buying anything. This is extremely important, simply because both of the other data mining techniques focus largely on those people who actually buy products from your company. In the first place, few casual shoppers will take the time to fill out a demographics survey, especially if they don't intend to buy anything, because your discount or freebie clearly doesn't apply to them. Transaction analysis, in the same vein, pertains only to actual customers for far more obvious reasons!

Click trails, however, serve the important role of helping you decide why people *leave* your site, or why they choose not to make a purchase. Indeed, knowing the exact path that visitors take through the site will highlight both the strengths and weaknesses of your store's organization.

- Do shoppers tend to bypass certain areas of your site?

- Which pages experience the heaviest traffic? The least?

- If a customer leaves your site, at which point is she most likely to "click off"?

- Is there any point at which visitors seem to become stuck or confused?

- Which link, if any, seems the most popular path to the online purchasing site?

Knowing which pages are unsuccessful can help you streamline the overall organization of your store. If you discover that a relatively large number of visitors leave immediately after having seen your homepage, you might want to redesign it! Likewise, if people seem to follow a roundabout route to checkout, or even frequently abandon their shopping carts, you should probably give the purchasing links a greater degree of prominence. You don't want to lose business because of a poorly designed site, and once you've officially launched your store, click trails are the best way to tinker with and continually improve the structure.

Data Mining and Customer Support

Data mining is certainly a powerful tool in the development and maintenance of your Web site. It helps you run an efficient, organized store that serves the needs of your customers. But what about one-on-one customer support? All the trends in the world can't help when you are confronted with an individual, someone with unique tastes and wants. To this effect, your company needs to employ relational databases that can single out the profile of each customer. Such a capability is a huge aid to the sales and marketing staff when they deal with customer problems on a personal level. When a customer calls, your company would be able to print out—among other things—his purchasing history, balance statement, a summary of any previous contact, and which links the customer prefers. All of this information can help salespeople handle customers' needs and concerns, and it can all be available at the touch of a button. Such data even applies when the client comes to your bricks-and-mortar store. Your site's daily Web activity is a wealth of information—don't fail to take advantage of it.

....

Regardless of your business size and goals, you must employ some form of data analysis. It's the best way to monitor the progress (or nonprogress) of your Internet venture—otherwise, all you've got to go on are gross figures and educated guesswork. Remember that e-commerce demands that companies be flexible; but you can't adapt if you can't keep track of changing conditions! Buy the software yourself if you haven't already purchased it, and have your IT staff set it up. If your company happens to outsource its online purchasing site, make sure that your turnkey will provide detailed feedback for your review. They may run the day-to-day operations of the site, but you can and should be involved in its design.

Maintain a Fast Connection

With the increasing emphasis on speed in the business world, it's no wonder that people are scrambling to help their stores sustain a breakneck pace. Internet pages should load quickly, and your store should try to ensure that transactions are fulfilled immediately—all to appease the speed-hungry Web shopper. But if you want your online store to be quick, you can't stop with the actual pages themselves. *Everyone* directly connected to your company must be able to keep up—and that includes your employees. Your internal Internet access thus becomes a critical issue. Even if you already have all employees "plugged in," is their connection as efficient as it could be? Enter the current leaders in business Internet access.

ISDN: Beloved of Small Business

The most basic of businesses, usually the so-called "garage-based" companies, sometimes connect to the Web with standard, consumer POTS technology. ("POTS," short for Plain Old Telephone Service, simply means that the modem will actually call up the local server number, just like a phone—which is why you hear the clicks and beeps as it connects over the established phone lines.) This is the type of modem that home surfers normally use, including most of your customers. Then, a few years ago, programmers came up with the Integrated Services Digital Network—or ISDN—option. Techno-jargon name aside, ISDN has been very popular with smaller businesses. Although it requires a normal dial-up, it relies on digital signals rather than the old analog kind. It allows the transfer of information at twice the rate of a civilian connection. Because it offers such an improvement, most companies have made the switch from standard service.

Frame Relay: The Big Business Option

Larger corporations have an option that far outranks ISDN. Frame relay, first of all, does not require standard dial-up connections. When you use a normal service, you are usually kicked off after a certain period of inactivity. Because of this, employees who surf the Web are required to log on and off several times a day, which wastes time. Frame relay, however, provides dedicated access, which allows a user to log on and remain online—until he either chooses to close the application or physically shuts his computer down. Being able to make immediate transfers between the Internet and normal programs is invaluable, for obvious reasons. And yet, a perpetual connection is only part of the story. Frame relay also allows for data transfer at up to *twenty-five times* the rate of the not-inadequate ISDN! The potential is amazing—and yet only the largest companies have been taking advantage of the frame relay option. Why? The oldest story in the book—it's incredibly expensive.

DSL: The Upstart Challenger

DSL is the perfect option for almost any smaller business.

Nevertheless, progress marches on. In recent months, a new option has debuted to the joy of small companies all over the world: DSL. DSL— digital subscriber line—provides the dedicated access and high speeds that frame relay offers, but it does so at bargain-basement prices. It can also support a number of users on the same connection; it can't match the sheer bulk of frame relay, but smaller companies don't require that much space anyhow. DSL can provide for anywhere from one to about twenty-eight constant users—and almost *twice* that upper limit if the users are occasional. Such numbers include plenty of bandwidth for most growing businesses, many of which are now rejoicing that they can approach the speeds of conglomerate giants. Viva technology! Definitely consider using DSL for your company's online venture, particularly if you're currently on standard dial-up or ISDN. You've got to move quickly to be competitive, and DSL can help you swim with the big fish.

DSL is actually a general type of access, under which many sub-categories exist: ADSL (the most common), CDSL, RDSL, HDSL, IDSL, VDSL, and more. For now, you needn't concern yourself with distinguishing among the types—they all embody the DSL qualities discussed above. To make referencing simple, when people refer to DSL in general, they often call it xDSL, with the "x" representing all of the different first letters.

Bluetooth: The Future of Internet Access?

Amusingly, even as corporate men and women celebrate the advent of DSL, technology has already advanced to the point where the physical connections themselves may soon be rendered unnecessary. Computer technology is rapidly shedding the traditional restraints of wires and cables—certain cell phones can now access the Internet, albeit on a limited basis. Still, at the current rate of progress, it won't be too long before mobile Internet access is a practical reality. Enter Bluetooth.

Bluetooth is a system that relies on shortwave radio signals to link electronic devices. Although it is currently still in the testing stages, when it becomes widely available users will be able to free themselves of the traditional electronic leashes. Since it uses radio signals to connect to special Bluetooth terminals, cables are simply unnecessary. So how does it work? Basically, all computers that contain a special microchip will be able to communicate with one another over a designated radio frequency. They will be able to share files and send messages without having to plug in. Each personal computer can also manage wireless access to the Web through one of the Bluetooth terminals. The prototype models have an admittedly short range of about thirty feet, yet the implications are still enormous. The technology is incredibly cheap; the card necessary for a personal computer will likely start at a price of less than $200. It's also a universal product— Bluetooth can work in a wide variety of computer brands and appliances. Thousands of corporations have already signed on to implement the system. So now we sit and wait to see what happens. Even as this book goes to press, the first commercial models are expected to be on the market. Will Bluetooth replace DSL almost before the latter gets off the ground? That remains to be seen!

Buy Your Supplies Online

Be adventurous! If you're going online, go all the way!

Now that you're planning to launch an Internet presence, it probably makes sense for you to integrate your current operations with the new technology as fully as possible. If you currently obtain supplies for your company through a traditional medium, such as catalog or phone ordering, you should consider moving the process online. In past years, online procurement was a bit complex—a business needed to construct its own interfaces to accept the sites of various vendors, which is a costly and cumbersome process. Now, all businesses with a private Intranet have a superior option, thanks to the OBI standard.

OBI, short for Open Buying on the Internet, is a set of rules and regulations that govern business-to-business online transactions. It provides for a standard electronic structure of ordering applications, so that companies can easily host any number of preferred vendors on their own Intranet. There's no need to provide for the creation of an endless number of unique interfaces, which frees companies to offer a wide variety of options to their employees without paying a heavy price.

Employees who engage in procurement over the Intranet have a fairly simple task. They must first select a category of products—for example, office supplies, raw materials, etc. The Intranet then exhibits the online catalog of the appropriate preferred vendor, the employee shops, makes a choice, and submits his order. The vendor then sends the request back to the proper authority for approval, and upon receiving official sanction, the order is filled and shipped. Instead of spending weeks languishing in endless paperwork, an order can be requested and received within a few days.

Online ordering is an excellent option for growing companies; it reduces overhead costs by a great deal, and it also helps novice employees become comfortable with the Internet. If you have a functional Intranet, it's hard to go wrong with this particular technology.

Site Maintenance

The upkeep of an online store is a serious, full-time concern. Maintaining Web sites is rather like caring for a delicate plant—they require constant attention and pruning, or they will wither and die. If you ignore your storefront for more than a day, it can quickly become outdated, cluttered with dead links, and will drive away customers who are looking for fresh material. It is therefore of the utmost importance that you preserve the relevance and organization of your store long after it opens its doors for the first time.

To this effect, you should probably hire one person to be in charge of site maintenance—a person usually referred to as the "Webmaster." Depending on the size of your company, this employee could either be the sole person assigned the duty or the head of a larger department. Only the tiniest companies with simple sites should allow anyone to work on the virtual store part-time. Either way, *somebody* should have clear authority. Never appoint a committee in which everyone holds equal power—that's a sure way to promote in-fighting and an incoherent storefront. Online stores demand an aura of consistency, and the only way to ensure a consistent appearance is to have a single individual in charge of the site content. Your Webmaster should be careful to preserve the following things:

Valid Links

As mentioned in Chapter 4, dead links are a major source of irritation to Web surfers. If you are planning to provide links to external sites, the Webmaster should check them all at frequent intervals, to ensure that all are valid. If an outside site changes its address, the Webmaster should either find and incorporate the new URL or remove the link. He should also try to avoid changing the URL of your own internal pages; visitors who use a search engine would not be affected, but your valuable frequent customers would be irritated if their bookmark for your page were to become invalid.

Current Information

Anything outdated or relatively old should be immediately discarded. This includes the obvious, such as "upcoming events" that have already passed or sales that happened last weekend—but it also includes the gray areas. The meaning of the word "current" will depend largely on the business of your company and the volume of your customer traffic. Any site devoted to technological concerns should have fresh content and news every single day. A small store that sells afghans could probably get away with weekly or bi-weekly updates. Keep in mind, however, that it's best to err on the side of frequent changes. New content helps beget increased traffic, since customers won't want to miss anything. If you go for months without altering the "What's New?" page, visitors will be unable to find a compelling reason to patronize your store. How often would you go to the movies if they kept re-running the same old six films?

Consistency

The Webmaster should also work to preserve the color schemes and page templates that were implemented at the outset. All new pages should be okayed by the Webmaster before they are posted. The ideal store should look unified, as though it were created entirely by one person. This is relatively easy in a small site, but larger virtual stores can become surprisingly eclectic in appearance. Despite the value of variety in some settings, consistency in appearance is vital to your store's professional image. Make sure everything appears cut from the same cloth.

A Logical Flow of Information

As successful Web sites blossom, a relatively simple store may swell to include hundreds of pages within a very short span of time. When unchecked by a governing hand, a gigantic tangle of new Web pages will glut your store and clog up the works. In order to function, all

Web sites need to preserve a logical flow of information, usually starting with the general and proceeding to the more specific. If your product information pages list items that have been slapped on without regard to category, customers will find it difficult to get what they want. This is extremely irritating. Similarly, if a shopper clicks through a series of pages only to become lost, she will want to see a prominently displayed link that can return her instantly to the homepage. Unfortunately, if several people are independently working to expand the site, these are exactly the kinds of situations that can arise. Newly created sub-subcategories can arise in the strangest places, where no ordinary shopper might think to look. A Webmaster's job is to oversee and design all additions to a Web site—with one person in charge of structure, your store is less likely to appear disorganized or fragmented.

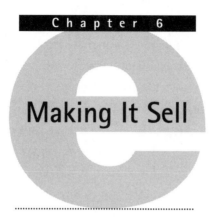

Chapter 6

Making It Sell

Hundreds of quality online ventures are currently struggling to stay financially afloat. Although they offer desirable products in an attractive format, they nevertheless have trouble building a steady flow of customer traffic. Why? Often, it's because they have not been working hard enough or creatively enough to build a customer awareness of their sites. In the real world, a new store can simply hang a banner and hope to attract the interest of those drivers who pass the business each day. It can also print flyers and post them around town—or place an ad in the newspaper. All of these time-honored techniques are helpful when used in the real world. But on the Internet, suddenly the old rules no longer apply. Just as managers have to adapt to a new style of business, so they must accept new forms of advertising.

141

....

Having an established real-life presence does *not* exempt you from the need to advertise!

....

At least your business will launch with a solid head start. You already have an established clientele, so it will be easy to notify your regulars about the new online face of your store. But if you really desire Internet success, you have to stretch beyond your existing comfort zone. Besides, there's no guarantee that your current customers will even *want* to shop at your Web store; even those who do might not constitute sufficient numbers to make your site profitable. It is extremely important, therefore, not to rely on existing customers for the livelihood of your Internet venture. In fact, that's one of the main mistakes that bricks-and-mortar companies make. Know this, then: You can't work ridiculously hard to produce a quality product, then kick back and wait for things to take care of themselves.

If you want your Web store to succeed, you must take the initiative.

So ready yourself for action. The job's not finished yet!

Real Life Advertising Strategies

Word of Mouth

It's really easy to forget about one of the most effective—and oldest—ad techniques around: word of mouth. Your site can get a great deal of mileage out of simple customer referrals. If one customer likes your site, she'll tell a few friends, who will try it and spread the word further, etc. This is naturally an advantage for the bricks-and-mortar manager—a solid number of people already know and trust your company! Nevertheless, your customers are only familiar with your real life store; they might not even be aware that you're building an online site. So it's up to you to spread the gospel. Tell *every* customer you see about the Web site. Talk it up, emphasize its convenience and any other benefit of your particular store. Start way in advance, and try to get everyone excited about the expected opening date.

Never, ever underestimate the power of buzz! Word-of-mouth is actually the most common way visitors find a Web site, even ahead of the Internet's most powerful search engines. Your customers are your best cheerleaders—if you leave them out in the cold, you're passing up an incredible opportunity to promote the site.

- **Offer Coupons.** Begin giving bricks-and-mortar customers coupons with every purchase from your store. Naturally, these discounts should be valid only on your Web site! Giveaways and freebies are a great way to get those with lukewarm interest to stop procrastinating and stop by for a look at the new, online you.

- **Update Your Business Cards.** Your business cards should all include your company's URL, in addition to your own corporate e-mail address. If you pass these out to customers, they'll be able to remember exactly where you're located! It makes it easier for them to find you online, and it also helps keep your new venue fresh in their memories. New bricks-and-mortar customers should be able to tell immediately that you run an online store—it shouldn't come as a surprise to them on their fourth or fifth visit.

- **Advertise While They Wait.** If you have the capability to place your customers on hold when you are on the phone with them, take advantage of the dead time they spend sitting around waiting. Pre-record and play a message that describes your company and its new Web site. They might as well listen while they wait. Just remember to keep it brief and rotate the message on a regular basis. Nobody wants to hear the same recording for five years. Update it as conditions change at your company. Whatever you do, though, do not prolong their wait on hold just so they can hear the recording. Waiting on hold is one of the least favorite—if not *the* least favorite—customer experiences.

Flyers

Flyers are *not* the world's greatest advertising technique.
Avoid them if you can.

Passing out flyers is an old trick, but it can be useful in its own way. You can print up sheets of paper advertising the company, and post them in public places, pass them out to people on the street, or put them under car windshield wipers in parking lots. It will help boost awareness of your venture.

Nevertheless, flyers do have a few drawbacks. For one thing, many people think that they're really tacky, not to mention inconsiderate. They hate it when they start to drive away, then have to stop and pull a brightly colored sheet of paper off the windshield. Some might even make a point to *not* go to your store if they're irritated enough. Besides, passing out flyers is extremely time consuming—if you can't spare the staff hours, don't do it.

You also want to stay away from flyers if you are aiming at a niche market. If you are already successful as a niche retailer, then you have probably come close to saturating the market in your particular geographical area. After all, if you make a good living in Boise selling vintage copies of Lord Byron's poetry, then you can rest assured that virtually everyone nearby who would be interested is probably already a regular customer. You can save time and energy just by notifying these people as they visit your store. Niche businesses should focus on expanding their market in *other* areas—maybe you can aim for those untapped reserves of Byron-lovers in Phoenix, Arizona. To that end, you should try print ads.

• **National Publications.** Print ads are an excellent option for those niche retailers looking to attract customers that were too far afield for the bricks-and-mortar store. You can post advertisements in trade journals, special interest magazines, newsletters, or any other print media that focus on your target market. If you haven't ever offered a mail-order service, opening an online store is an incredible opportunity for you to greatly expand your clientele.

- **Local Publications.** Other, more "wide-appeal" types of businesses such as general crafts stores or home grocers should also take advantage of local advertising opportunities. You can run ads in the local paper or other regional publications, thus spreading the word to all those who live close by. This method naturally works best for those companies that perform a service: house painters, maid services, DJs, plumbers, etc. These people would *need* to confine themselves to a designated geographical area—the very nature of their companies demands it. Why advertise to people whom you cannot serve?

Notify the Media

Advertisements aren't the only way to spread the word. Journalists can do much of the initial work for you, completely free of charge! When your site is nearing completion, have your marketing department prepare a press release for the media. What do you say in a press release? Such reports announce to news sources (and by extension, the public) that your company has moved online.

> Press releases are great because they seem more like news than advertisements.

Good press releases have a powerful sense of purpose. They should be focused and concise, with a length of no more than a thousand words. They're supposed to be highly digestible, not explain the history of your company in exhaustive detail: Why should the public visit your virtual store? What advantages do you offer that no other competing business can? If you tell a compelling enough story, the media will run coverage of your debut. Even better, if you write it in a professional, journalistic fashion, the editor may even choose to run the release word-for-word! Just make sure that you preserve a subtle tone; this is supposed to be a news story, not an ad.

So where should you send it? Focus on reaching niche markets. Even if *The New York Times* won't care about your small company, you might find interested parties via trade journals, special interest magazines, local newspapers, or others. Sending a press release is free, so try anyone else who could conceivably be interested. You can call a newspaper or magazine in advance to procure the name of the editor, or whoever else might be in charge of press releases. If you can address it directly to him, then your statement probably won't be lost in the limbo between departments. People often respond positively to business write-ups. Since the information comes from an unbiased third party, people are less likely to dismiss you outright.

Press releases are simply more effective than print ads. The downside, of course, is that they should only be used once—during your Grand Opening. A word of warning: Never, ever issue a press release until your site is functional. Certain types of advance advertising are desirable, but once newspapers and magazines report your existence, you need to be up and running. If your statement is ready in advance, then ask the publication to hold the release until a certain date. Put this information in an upper corner of the page, so that it won't be mistakenly run ahead of schedule. For example, simply add: "Please hold until 06/29/01."

Virtual Advertising Strategies

Put a "Construction Sign" on the Future Site

Before you go online, while your shopping and/or purchasing sites are still being designed and built, you should post a simple business card–quality sign at your address. Although not many people may be visiting your site at this point, at least you can generate a little buzz. And, if you can get listed on a search engine, a few people may stumble on the store, become intrigued, and come back after you open for a more thorough look.

Your construction sign should include the following information:

1. The company name
2. Your real-life address
3. Your phone, fax, and e-mail contact information
4. A brief description of your company and products and/or services
5. The expected opening date of the online store

With a little luck, you might even be able to bring in some added business to your bricks-and-mortar store as well. Customers who live in your geographical area might decide to pay a visit to the physical store. After all, a site this simple costs you virtually nothing. If it can add to your business in the slightest, then it's worth it.

Search Engines

The easiest and most important way to advertise your store on the Web is to register it with every major search engine. Almost any customer who runs a search will stick to the options provided in the list of results—and if you're not there, they'll likely try one of your competitors. And who uses search engines? Everybody! Contrary to popular opinion, search engines aren't just for Internet newcomers. According to a CommerceNet/Nielson study, over 70 percent of frequent Web users try a search engine *first* when looking for a site. Registering your online store with search engines is simply nonnegotiable. All search engines function in their own manner, but there are actually two types of Web search companies: true search engines, and directories. Directories will be discussed later.

> To register with a true search engine, all you really need is a little patience and a comfy chair!

Registering with a true search engine could actually be called "the passive approach." Believe it or not, many search engines, such as Alta Vista, Excite, or WebCrawler, are actually willing to do the "searching" themselves! In order to keep their listings up-to-date, such companies deploy devices called "robots," "bots," or "spiders"— depending on whom you're talking to. Spiders automatically comb the entire World Wide Web, looking for key words and phrases to help the program place the various pages and sites in an accurate context. They then transmit the information back to their host, which soon places it in an "index."

Once there, your site will be accessible to the search software— and you didn't even need to lift a finger! Still, letting the spiders "crawl" your site on their own is not a good idea. Their methods are automated, which means that they can't consider context when classifying your business site. Many Web crawlers will read only the first several lines of text on your page, then make a decision based solely on that information. So, if your site does not prominently post the words most relevant to your business, you could wind up at the bottom of search lists. That's very bad. Most Web surfers will only check the top twenty listings for any given search, so if your company ranks 312th, your chances of being seen are pretty dismal. If you want to survive, you should make a definite effort to elbow your way into the top two result pages—but you'll have to be patient. Competition for a high ranking usually entails a high degree of perseverance accompanied by old-fashioned trial and error.

For one thing, you'll need to post relevant phrases, which unfortunately poses quite a challenge. The mechanisms by which engines rank Web sites are both diverse and complex; an element that might improve your standings at Infoseek may actually harm you when the Excite spiders visit. The best approach is to adhere to the most common strategies and to *not* obsess over the details.

- **Word Placement.** Search engine programmers generally design spiders to place the most emphasis on the top part of your Web page. The logic is fairly obvious: The more important the keyword is to your site, the higher up it's likely to be. After all, if you sell curtains and Venetian blinds, you'll post phrases relevant to these topics near the top of your page rather than discuss lamps or end tables. To this end, you'll want to do some serious thinking about which words are most important to your site. If *you* were shopping for the goods or services your store provides, what word combinations would you try at the search engine? Take this step seriously—choosing keywords is a marketing issue, so don't let your IT people make the decision on their own. If your most important words are too vague, you might show up as only one of thousands on the results list. Pretend that you run a sports-hobby shop. "Basketball" or "cars" would not be good choices for the top of your homepage: The first example would dredge up all ten jillion NBA and NCAA sites, and "cars" would include actual manufacturers. Instead, try using "basketballs" or "model cars" in the description of your store. These phrases are much more limited in scope, and thus would be more likely to match you with customers interested in your products, not the latest sports news.

Choose your words carefully. They will have a big impact
on your site rankings.

Once you know which keywords are best, post them as high as possible on your homepage. The spiders will then see them as having more relevance than information near the bottom—and this will, in turn, result in a better ranking. Also beware of placing graphics or pictures at the top of your page. Spiders can't take these features into account; they can scan only standard text. Graphics, then, serve only to shove your all-important introductory paragraph farther down the page—and search engines *will* notice that displacement!

• **Word Repetition.** Search engines will also consider word repetition when indexing any Web site. Again, this is no surprise. Programmers are simply operating on the reasonable assumption that the more times a Web site repeats a word or phrase, the more relevant it must be. If you sell different kinds of used books, you would probably use that phrase more than once on your homepage—more minor topics would only be mentioned once, if at all.

Clever word placement and repetition will help direct potential customers to your site; they provide you with both higher rankings *and* a more accurate description of your site on the search engine listings. Still, you should remember and accept that rankings are not an exact science. Each engine's individual criteria will differ at least slightly from the others'. Directories, especially, will vary from company to company—they rank sites at least partly according to the involved employee's personal opinion! Because of this, choosing keywords is not always an easy task.

The complexity is only increased for stores that sell a wide variety of services or products. They may have difficulty attracting customers looking for specific types of items. Although people normally check for broad categories in the real-life Yellow Pages, Web surfers can (and do) commence their searches with a mind-boggling array of keywords. If you run a small plant nursery, you want the engines to pick up your site for shoppers in pursuit of anything from azaleas to zinnias. Yet if a particular customer is looking for roses, she'll likely enter "roses" as a keyword—not "gardening" or "flowers." After all, the savvy shopper knows that there are plenty of sites on the Web that specialize in one kind of bloom. Thus, if the top section of your site fails to mention roses, the Web engines will skip your site when processing that request, and such a customer will never even see your store. This poses a potential problem. How can your business possibly post every important keyword on the page without winding up with a cluttered, unreadable site?

Many companies experience difficulty listing all of their business topics at the top of the page—at least, without looking ridiculous. On the homepage of a nursery, for example, you should post a well-written introduction to the business. Yet at the same time, you want spiders to notice all major facets of your company. This is a problem; you don't want your first few lines of text to read like a boring shopping list, but neither can you risk skipping a mention for an important item. If you place roses at the top of your page, then mustn't you also list every shrub, vine, climber, perennial, and hothouse variety? Not necessarily. Meta tags are a tidy solution.

- **Meta Tags.** Meta tags are special lines of HTML code that only spiders can read; they don't show up on a normal page view. Your company can therefore create a shopping list of your most important product categories without tiring the consumers. There are two main types of meta tags—keyword and description. Both of these are normally placed directly under the official title bar of the homepage. For your nursery, the code might look somewhat like this:

<META NAME="keywords" CONTENT="gardening, gardens, nursery, plants, shrubs, vines, roses, pansies, daffodils, begonias, sunflowers, violets">

<META NAME="description" CONTENT="Summer's Nursery grows and sells the best organic flowers and shrubs in the Northwest. We're proud to announce that all of our plants thrive on sunshine, fresh water, and pure mountain air—not artificial chemicals or pesticides. We also provide fast service at competitive prices: Summer's Nursery can match you with the perfect, healthy plant within forty-eight hours of your order.">

Keyword meta tags are completely invisible to the average Web surfer. The top lines serve as a statement of content only to the Web crawlers; they ensure that search engines will notice your most important keywords. The description tag, on the other hand, *will* be seen by prospective customers.

Make sure you write a good description tag. It's what the engine will post in the search listings.

Although only spiders can read the description tag on your site, they will recycle it as the blurb used when your site is listed in a search. You can thus make certain that when a customer pulls up a list of various nurseries during the course of a search, your store will be represented in your own words. If you fail to design a description tag, the engine will just automatically post the first few lines of text from your page instead. This is far less convenient, since you would have to design your page with the knowledge that the top lines might be clumsily copied out of context, and indexed by any passing search engine. Meta tags offer your site a solid degree of creative control.

A word of warning, however. Not surprisingly, soon after their introduction certain virtual stores began to misuse meta tags. In some cases, they would list literally *hundreds* of keywords, trying to cover *every* conceivable item in stock. In other instances, stores would constantly repeat the same phrase, in hopes that repetition would lead to a high placement on the resulting search list. This act, also known as "spoofing," is particularly reprehensible to true engines, since it deliberately seeks to undermine the painstakingly programmed spiders. Search companies do not look kindly on such flagrant abuses, and now have ways of circumventing such posts—they may even punish such offenses. If an engine feels that their services are being used inappropriately, most will remove the offending URL from their listings. There's no better punishment; not surprisingly, shunning is the most effective way to wound a publicity-hungry Web site. Such rampant fraud quickly emphasized the need for reform, so today the major engines are focused more on overall page content than on meta tags. All in all, it's a good idea to make use of tags, but do not rely solely on them to promote your site.

....

Careful planning is the best way to ensure that your Web site finds a good ranking on search lists. Nevertheless, whether you take the initiative or not, your store will eventually end up somewhere on the indices of search engines. Strategy may be important, but just getting crawled by spiders requires no effort at all. Yet the term "search engine" is used in a generic sense on the Internet; not all companies referred to as such are actually search engines in the strictest sense of the word.

- **Web Directories.** Web directories, to the consumer, are virtually indistinguishable from true search engines: Their purpose is still to provide lists of relevant sites when a visitor enters a few key words or phrases. The difference is in the way they gather information—directories such as Yahoo! do not employ automated spiders to rake up reams of data. Instead, they catalog Web sites on a purely voluntary basis.

> If you modify the URL or content of your Web site, don't forget to notify all Search Directories of the change.

In order to get listed on a Web directory, someone has to put in a formal request at the directory's main site. The directory will then have the applicant fill out a form, which usually includes a request for a brief descriptive paragraph about the candidate site. (Just as search engines use description meta tags, directories normally use these self-reported lines in search listings.) After you have completed the paperwork, the directory will then categorize the site according to this data—*and nothing else*. If you make any substantial changes in your Web site, don't expect the directory to find out. They'll never actually see, or "crawl" your site as the spiders do, so if you need to account for modifications, you'll have to contact the directory yourself.

Both search engines and Web directories are free services—they make their money through advertising—so there's no excuse not to take advantage of the opportunity. Make sure that your site is listed at *all* of the top ten to fifteen search companies:

Yahoo!	Lycos	Alta Vista	WebCrawler	Infoseek
Excite	Hotbot	Netscape	Snap.com	Ask Jeeves
AOL.com	MSN	Magellan	GoTo	LookSmart

Will this be time-consuming? Not necessarily. Several existing companies will mass-register you with a large number of search engines, either for free or for a small flat fee. Register It is free, Submit It and WorldSubmit charge a negligible amount of money. (WorldSubmit charges only nine dollars to register you with 100 different search engines.) If you don't have the time or inclination to individually visit and apply at each of the above search engine sites, visit one of these companies. Either way, no matter how you look at it, publicly posting your URL is incredibly simple—and cheap!

Banners

Banners are the rectangular ad images or graphics that appear independently at the top or bottom of countless popular Web pages. While a normal page is downloading, they pop up quickly on the screen, catching the shopper's eye and promoting the sponsor business. Far beyond being mere signposts, however, banners are also *direct* links to the advertiser's Web site. If a surfer is sufficiently intrigued by the banner, he can click on it to instantly move to the advertiser's own homepage!

> Banners allow surfers to respond instantly to the advertisement—which makes them far more effective.

Banners are currently the most popular form of advertising on the Internet, and for good reason. In the first place, they offer instant gratification to Web surfers. That's important—customers are most responsive to marketing immediately after they see the ad. Traditional advertising requires the shopper to negotiate a series of hurdles in order to respond. Even in the case of virtual stores, the customer must remember the URL, go home, and actually log on. Quite frankly, by that point most people don't care anymore. The power of such marketing strategies is thus greatly diluted by the number of steps involved in responding to the ad. And, since the follow-through entails so much persistence, potential customers who are only vaguely interested will probably just forget about making the effort.

Banner ads solve this problem. By marketing online, the customer can respond to the ad with one click of the mouse—and be directly transported to the sponsor's Web site. The convenience of banners thus allows advertisements to attract a far larger pool of customers than ever thought possible!

Another advantage of banner ads is the high degree of control they offer companies. Traditional print ads are difficult to adjust or remove once in circulation. If a business wants to improve an existing ad, it must wait until a new edition of the publication is distributed—and this can take months! Banner ads, on the other hand, can be posted for virtually any length of time. Sponsor companies are free to tinker with or update their banners whenever they feel like it. If, after a few days, a marketing expert finds that a certain ad is not successful, she can replace it with a new version within hours. Such an opportunity allows the advertising "evolutionary" process to happen at a quicker pace. Unsuccessful banners can be yanked before they become costly mistakes. All that's required of the company is a certain degree of vigilance.

So what should a good banner include? That's a hard question to answer. They come in so many sizes and forms that it's difficult to generalize. What kind will work best for you? Make sure to consider the following categories.

- **Placement.** Banners are usually placed at either the top or bottom of a page, and can cover the entire width of the screen. (In fact, their traditionally narrow, rectangular shape is what earned them the "banner" moniker.) Nevertheless, they can appear in other places as well—including the sides of the page. These upright banners even have a special name; they're referred to as "in-line ads." Still, no matter where they appear, banners are almost always far from the center of the page. Not surprisingly, they're confined to the extremities in order to prevent them from interfering with the actual page content.

  Banners actually come in a wide variety of sizes—you'll need to decide which ones will work best for your ad campaign.

- **Size.** Contrary to the stereotype, banners are not uniform in dimension. Most are still full-sized, but they are becoming increasingly available in smaller versions. When you buy a banner, you'll have to stipulate which size you want. This is measured in two different ways. Some companies do a pixel count to determine size, with the average banner running at about 400 long × 40 pixels wide. The Internet Advertising Bureau (IAB) stipulates full-size versions to be 468 by 60—but not all Web sites follow this standard. Other companies classify ads through file size, usually setting the maximum at about 7.5KB, since the amount of information the ad carries determines the loading time of a banner—which is, remember, a very important consideration on the Internet.

Regardless of which method is used, try to adhere to the good old rule of moderation. Extremely large ads may attract attention, but they take a longer time to download. If customers are impatient about just waiting for your actual Web pages to load, imagine how dismal your chances will be with a slow-moving, unsolicited advertisement! They're also more expensive; companies will charge more for larger dimensions. On the other hand, smaller, cheaper banners are simply less likely to catch the eye of passing visitors, and what's the point of advertising if nobody notices? In the end, there is no one right answer. Your decision should take into account your company's unique situation—its finances as well as its needs.

- **Content.** Most banner ads are currently a mix of plain text and simple graphics, with click-throughs hinging upon the efficacy of the actual message the banner conveys. You'll want to spend some serious time considering the content of each banner your company creates; if you can afford it, you probably want to entrust a professional ad agency with the assignment. After all, using a cramped space to convince visitors to detour unexpectedly—just to check out your store—is no easy task!

  A quick search on the Web will reveal dozens of companies who are willing to design your banner for you. Their services can cost anything from virtually nothing to hundreds of dollars, but as usual, don't jump at the cheapest deal. Ask to see some examples of their work, and shop around until you feel comfortable with a particular business. Since it'll be representing you in a *very* public manner, you need to make sure that the designers will do a quality job. If you decide to create the banners yourself, there are a couple of options. Off-the-shelf software packages contain design templates—you can usually buy one for less than $100, but you'll need to put the "pieces" together in coherent fashion. There are also online do-it-yourself sites that allow you to create the image of a banner; they then commit it to code and deliver the finished product. Just remember that it might take an amateur a very long time to come up with a great banner. Trial and error can be extremely time-consuming, so don't underestimate the real costs associated with doing it on your own.

Your banners should play on the curiosity of the visitor. Get them interested enough to click through.

Nevertheless, whoever creates your ads, stick to a few guiding principles: Most important, you need to grab the visitors' attention. Interesting colors or a good approach can help you get people to take a second look. Still, of those people who do check out the banner, only a very small percentage of passersby will actually click through—often because it involves a detour. Keep in mind that most Web surfers have an extremely short attention span, and they're impatient to boot. Give them an immediate, salient reason to visit your site. Why should they bother with your company? What can you offer them? Make your banner special by pushing a unique angle or saying something unexpected.

Your banners should not be boring mirror-images of your
print ads. Be sure to make use of the new technology—enjoy
what cyberspace has to offer!

Try to stay away from worn-out, standard catchphrases
like "Lowest Prices!" or "Win, win, win!" Nobody really expects
these to be true, and they might even make your site appear a bit
second-rate. You want your ads to be memorable, not a carbon
copy of some grandiose, empty junk mail promise. Also, make
sure that the site itself upholds the messages in your banners. If
a customer feels disillusioned once he visits the store, he won't
come back. So if you can't hit upon something catchy or unique,
at least keep it straightforward and honest. Don't forget to add
the universal prompt to "click here"—although the concept
seems painfully obvious to experienced surfers, some newer visitors don't know that banners are clickable images. It's better to
be safe than sorry! Nevertheless, more and more companies
have been trying to go beyond this meat-and-potatoes banner
approach; they understand that conventionality can be limiting.
It's extremely difficult to break new ground using banners with
pictures and text only; customers are growing ever harder to impress. So, knowing that many customers have become inured to
standard banners, some businesses have taken to including
other elements—namely, just about anything that will grab the
attention of passing Web surfers!

- **Animation.** Animation is a great tool to counteract visitor indif-
  ference, because it addresses the root cause: Web surfers
  quickly learn that the boxes around the edges of a page are almost always advertisements, so after a period of time they
  might stop noticing the banners at all. Like moviegoers in a
  darkened theater, they focus their attentions on the big screen,

not on their immediate surroundings. Animation helps mitigate this problem. Since it involves some sort of movement— whether flashing text or a brief dancing graphic—an animated banner is far more likely to catch shoppers' eyes. After all, in order to be swayed by your ad, they have to actually see it! Just know that the usual limits apply. You should try to keep the animation cycle under four seconds, or the graphic file will become unwieldy. If it loads too slowly, your potential customer may have explored the screen, made a choice, and moved on before your banner even materializes! Animation can be great, but until technology allows for faster loading, you'll want to use it sparingly.

- **Interactivity.** Animation isn't the only technique developed to help attract attention; creating an interactive banner is also a great way to draw in potential customers. Many sites have begun building forms into their banners—they solicit opinions on a topic of interest, provide a brief, free service, or offer to provide answers to customer questions. The forms, created with "rich media" technology, allow for immediate interaction; they are developed with object-oriented programming languages such as Java. Such banners enable customers to answer the queries in simple forms such as drop-down lists or radio buttons—*within the banner itself!* After providing a bit of feedback, the banner then usually invites the Web surfer to click through to the site for more information. These forms are more likely to generate customer interest, since they pique interest without requiring the surfer to commit to a new site. People are accustomed to passive, boring ads; they are simply more receptive when they're allowed to participate. If you run a tutoring service, you might provide a form that allows the shopper to enter the age of his child and the general subject(s) in which the kid needs help. Your banner would then prompt him to visit the site to learn more about your services for that age group and subject matter. Once they have invested some time in the ad, people are more likely to investigate further—that is, click through to your store!

- **Taglines.** Some Web pages will allow you to include a short phrase or sentence beneath your actual banner; these are called taglines. Taglines are a great resource if your banner could use any extra commentary. Instead of trying to cram your slogan into a crowded banner, you might merely reproduce it just below. Conversely, if your logo and slogan are used in the graphic, you can advertise a freebie or discount in the tagline: "10 Percent Off Your Entire Purchase on Your First Visit!" Taglines are usually limited to somewhere between six and twelve words, and they are offered only if the host site chooses to do so. They're also more expensive, so if you don't really need a tagline, don't worry about making one.

- **Pop-ups.** In a related vein, advertisements can also load separately from the page itself—such devices are referred to as pop-up ads. When a user downloads a Web page, a pop-up appears in a window on top of the actual content. The advantage of pop-ups is that they force the customer to notice the ad, even if only to click it off. They also cover more space than a traditional banner, and so they can include a substantial amount of information. These two qualities usually cause pop-ups to have a higher success rate than normal banners. However, many customers find them highly annoying, since they appear on top of the actual page content and often seem to slow the entire loading process. Regular banners are generally perceived as harmless, so they're not seen in a very negative light. But pop-up ads often cause tempers to flare. Many surfers even seek out a program that destroys pop-ups in advance: Pop-Up Killer. Be very careful if you decide to use this type of ad—you may be alienating more people than you attract.

....

Pop-ups can be an incredible waste of money, but they can
also be wildly successful—it's a calculated risk.

....

Once you've created a viable banner or two, you can start looking around for places to post them. This is an incredibly important
step—all advertisements depend on their audience for success, so
you *must* choose a good audience. If you place an ad for your hardware
store at the Baby Gap site, you'll see far fewer click-throughs than if
you market your store to a carpentry discussion group! This is where
your target audience truly comes into play, especially if you aren't
catering to a particular niche interest. Do some quality research, and
find out which Web sites are most popular with your market segment.
When approaching a possible host for your banner, ask them about
their demographics and other statistical data. Don't pay for an advertisement to be displayed where no one will care about it! You'll want
to start looking in one or more of a few major areas. Listed below are
various possibilities, ranging from specialized to general in scope.

- **Niche Stores.** Advertising in a niche store can be either extremely productive or a complete failure—but careful research
  can help you avoid the latter result. If your services and/or
  products are generally made for a very particular audience, then
  you should probably advertise heavily on the most popular
  sites for your target market. If you sell cigars, you'd naturally
  want to market them in locations where cigar lovers are most
  likely to go. Do some careful market research to find out which
  stores are heavily trafficked by likely customers. Some of the
  sites may be obvious, but others aren't necessarily linked directly to your products. Your cigar store may want to advertise
  on both cigar-related sites *and* the homepages of popular winer-
  ies. Also, make sure that your ad venues receive enough business to be worth the money; again, your banners are useless if
  nobody sees them.

- **Destination Locations.** Informational sites are often referred to as "destination locations," which means that Web surfers visit them specifically to get information. These people may or may not be intending to shop, but they are definitely motivated enough to actively seek out knowledge on a particular topic. Newsgroups, educational sites, hobby sites, and critics all fall into this broad category. They don't sell anything themselves, but they attract specific kinds of people—perhaps people who fit your target profile. As with niche marketing, try to find out which of these locations are most popular with your audience, then post a banner or two.

- **Niche Portals.** Niche portals attract more people than specific stores, thus increasing the pairs of eyeballs that might notice your banner. Yet they're still narrower in scope than major portals; they generally serve as launching sites for certain categories of Web surfers: There are business portals, portals focused on women, news portals, and so on. Nevertheless, there's a trade-off. These specialty portals attract a wider band of people, who may or may not be interested in your products. Portals are simply not as targeted as specific Web sites. Nevertheless, the reward of heavier traffic almost always outweighs the decrease in focus.

Major portals are the best place to advertise—but they're also the most expensive.

- **Major Portals.** Major portals, since they attract all kinds of people, are attractive advertising venues simply due to their substantial volume of traffic. If you advertise on Yahoo!, Excite, CompuServe, or other such cyberspace doorways, you'll likely find success just from sheer exposure to thousands of people per day. Although major portals may not especially attract your target market, they usually attract large enough numbers to more than make up for their scattered audience. Major portals are the best idea for those companies with a broad appeal—such as house painters, bookstores, or home delivery services.

Despite their general popularity, many portals have taken steps to improve business and make themselves more attractive to advertisers. Some will allow you to specify a particular location for your banner. In such "targeted advertising," your ad will be displayed only in a certain general category on the site—Entertainment, Sports, Weather, News, Business, etc. Although the service costs extra, your banners would be more focused on your store's best market, rather than scattered throughout the entire portal. Even better, many portals/search engines allow businesses to purchase keywords. The implications of this option are enormous: Not only do you receive the great publicity of being on a portal site, but the resulting traffic will consist entirely of those individuals who check a topic of your choice! The search engine only displays your banner when someone runs a search for your keyword; you'll receive a hand-crafted audience, far more likely to click through your banner than the general public—or even those who browse in your general category. Such a method combines the strengths of targeted advertising while avoiding the pitfalls of advertising on small niche sites: Your company can attract a decent amount of specialized traffic without confining your ads to the cyberspace boondocks. Major portals are thus working to provide the same benefits as niche portals, without the drawbacks; competition is not always a bad thing!

Once you've decided on several great locations, you'll need to bite the bullet and get ready to pay for ad space. Still, posting ads is not always expensive, although the most common method of posting Web ads is to simply pay another site to display your banner. Prices vary; how much you pay, and what you receive in return, depends entirely upon the situation.

Obviously, the most important factor for your own company is how many actual *purchases* result from visitors who clicked through the banner to your site. Working from this premise, some banner postings are arranged on a per-transaction basis: Every time a click-through results in an actual purchase, the sponsor pays the host site a pre-arranged flat fee or percentage of the sale. Other than that, the ad space is free.

Try to arrange payment on a click-through basis—it's the most cost-efficient option for you. Just don't be surprised if the host site says no!

Alternatively, a few companies are also willing to receive payment on a "click-through" basis; this means that your business only gets billed according to the number of people who actually click through the banner to your site, whether or not a sale results. This is an excellent arrangement for your store: If the ad is successful, then the increase in profits will more than make up for the advertising costs. If the banner flops, you won't need to pay much of anything. Unfortunately, this situation rarely occurs, and for an obvious reason: The terms are extremely unfavorable for the host company. Few people are willing to stake their profits on the quality of a different company. If the banner is poorly designed, or if the sponsor site itself fails, the host business is left holding an empty bag. Because click-through deals often produce such lopsided results, experts strongly advise online businesses to request other methods of payment. If you can broker such a bargain, go for it—but don't be surprised if nobody jumps at the offer.

So how to measure the traffic of a potential host site? This is a vital matter, since traffic is used both to gauge the popularity of a page and to keep track of how many people are exposed to a banner ad. Until recently, people most often spoke in terms of how many "hits" a site received in a set period of time; a hit refers to a single download of *any* element on a Web page. The hits are extremely easy for the server to keep track of, but they have one important drawback: They do not provide an accurate picture of how many people have actually visited the site. If a single page contains text, a few graphics, and an HTML instruction file, then the server would count four or five hits when only one viewer downloads the entire page. Thus, although convenience originally made hits the most popular means of traffic measurement, their inaccuracy has caused them to fall from favor.

Currently, the most common form of payment is measured in the number of "impressions" your ad receives. An impression is the term used to describe one download of a page, and thus can also be referred to as a *page view*. Companies generally find this to be the most equitable arrangement—the host charges your business according to the number of times somebody downloads and sees your ad. In the first place, it's a good deal for the advertiser. Your company won't be punished by a low-traffic site, stuck paying a lot of money for no publicity. Instead, you'll only pay for the actual number of people who get to see the banner. There's also protection for the host company—they get paid the full fee regardless of how the ad works out for you.

....
Don't be discouraged by single-digit CTRs. Very few ads score
more than 5 or 6 percent.
....

Keep in mind that a large number of page impressions does not necessarily ensure a large influx of visitors to your site. If the ad is poor, or if the audience is simply not interested, you'll still have to pay up. Try to keep your expectations realistic. The average banner ad achieves only about a *3 percent* CTR, or Click-Through Ratio. In other words, only about three people out of 100 who download the page will actually click on the banner. This is not a large number! Some companies have boasted CTRs of 20 to 30 percent on certain ads, but such cases are rare.

Low CTRs mean that you'll want to pay for a lot of impressions. If only a few people visit your store for every hundred downloads the banner receives, you'll need to purchase many, many impressions. Such payments are thus usually arranged on a cost-per-thousand (CPM) basis. The base price is set by the host company, and is usually fixed between $50 and $100. The actual number you choose to purchase depends both on your company's needs and on its bank account—but the amount can easily run into the hundreds of thousands.

An alternative form of billing rests on the actual length of time the host site displays the banner. This method is the most like traditional advertising arrangements, but it is also one of the least popular. Why? Because the number of days or weeks the site displays your banner is not meaningful, either to the host company or you. It cannot account for the actual size of the audience that views the ad, much less measure the number of people who actually respond. Although payments based on time still exist, e-commerce is quickly making the method obsolete. The CPM system is simply better.

Regardless of which arrangements you wind up accepting, remember to research potential host sites carefully before brokering a deal. Make sure that the site attracts sufficient traffic and the right kinds of people. Banners that pop up for a receptive audience will obtain far higher CTRs than those not directed at your target market.

No matter how wildly successful your banners become, having to pay for them still stinks. Then again, who ever said you'd have to *pay* for advertising? The Internet has made it practical for certain companies to promote themselves without spending a single dime for the privilege! You can accomplish this by participating in banner exchange programs.

Banner exchanges are a great option for small companies that need publicity yet can't afford to purchase substantial ad space on other sites. The simplest way to exchange ads is to contact another business and offer to display one of their banners if they post one of yours. The details of the deal can be negotiated on a case-by-case basis; if the other company attracts more traffic, you might have to advertise their banner for a longer time than they show yours, to make up for the deficit. Still, it's free! And, if you make the arrangements yourself, your company wields complete control over the types of ads your own site will display.

Banner exchanges are an effective, inexpensive way to advertise.

If you're looking for an easier approach, there are several companies on the Web that exist exclusively as middlemen in large-scale banner exchanges. If you register with one of these companies, they promise to post your banner on other sites in return for your agreement to display whatever ads they assign you. The good news is that you will be widely promoted and may even receive great discounts on otherwise expensive sites: portals, destination sites, and other heavily trafficked areas. It's a great start.

Naturally, there's a catch. Registering with an exchange company means that you lose a certain degree of control over your own site. Whatever the company sends you, you have to post. In addition, you don't get to handpick the sites on which you advertise, which could potentially lower your CTR. Before you sign over to a program, make sure you clearly understand their policies. How many ads will they expect you to display? Will you have room to run a couple of privately negotiated exchanges? What kinds of businesses do they deal with? Your company does not want to be saddled with tasteless ads, porn banners, or anything else that would negatively affect your company's professional image. The most popular exchange companies currently include LinkExchange, Ad-Xchange, and BannerSwap.

Once you've made the arrangements to fly your banners on various other pages, don't sit back and relax. Always be on the lookout for better hosts and cheaper deals—improvement is an unending process, not a specific goal. You also need to make sure that your ad campaign maintains a fresh look. Create several different banners, and retain only those that perform well. Be willing to generate new material—no single banner should be exhibited on the same site for more than two weeks. Visitors will soon stop noticing it, and it will lose its efficacy. Instead, see if the host sites are willing to change your old ads for new ones every so often. Most companies don't mind, but ask in advance anyway. "Stale" banners are a waste of space.

Finally, try to hit upon an appropriate length of time to display the banner; this can be a lot more difficult than it seems! In the first place, don't whisk it away too soon. Once you purchase ad space, you must make sure that you fill it for a reasonable period of time. Most surfers won't respond to an ad the first time they see it—only after they've been reminded a few times are they willing to click through. A clever banner and fresh material can help, but you'll also need to provide for a decent period of exposure. Yet despite the need to allow the ad time to sink in, you don't want to "overbuy" space by leaving it up for too long. If you post on a site where, say, a thousand people visit on a regular basis and only a few new people show up from time to time, posting the banner for six months will be a waste of your good money. The benefit from your ad will be used up in the first few weeks, as all the interested regular clients click through to your store. If you provide them with a great experience, they won't need the ad again—they'll return on their own. At this point, you'll have to accept that the other regular customers are probably not interested, and wouldn't visit your site if the banner flew until doomsday. The trickle of new people also will probably not include enough potential customers to warrant your continued expense. You need a *variety* of people to see your ads; if you've chosen a smaller host site, pull the banner once you begin to experience diminishing returns. Other than that, choose well-trafficked locations that include plenty of fresh pairs of eyes every day.

For all their utility, banners are still strictly advertisements. They fail to create any kind of mutually beneficial partnership between the host company and the advertiser. Although the image of one company's banner might reflect indirectly on the host site, most customers will still view the two businesses as entirely separate. It's a purely superficial connection, and based on profit—not a similarity of content. Yet there are ways of establishing a deeper, longer-term relationship with another company. If you are interested in creating a more substantial bond, you might consider inviting another business to be an affiliate.

Affiliate Programs

Affiliate relationships generally occur between companies that are related in a tangential way. The involved businesses can create any sort of mutually beneficial relationship, but in cyberspace the agreement is usually geared towards customer referrals. So how does it work? Assuming that your own company is not a large conglomerate, the company you approach will usually be a larger entity. Your business offers to provide a link to the other company's site, and in return they give you a certain percentage or commission for each sale that results from the link. If your store, for example, sells surfboards, you might approach a popular online beachwear company. If they agree to the arrangement, you would then provide a link to the clothing store on your site, perhaps with a small tagline: "Need a new wetsuit? Try Duke's Swimwear." Since ISPs can track the source of each purchase, you would then receive a small fee for each customer who spends money at the affiliate site.

Don't affiliate with a direct competitor—if your customers click through the link, they might not come back!

Such a partnership can be lucrative for both companies, provided that they don't engage in direct competition! Beachwear, scuba equipment, or boat companies are good potential affiliates for a surfboard vendor, but make sure they don't sell items that your own company offers. Obviously, you should not provide links to other companies that sell surfboards. If your visitor likes the other company's banner and clicks over, he might find a better model on the other Web site. Don't shoot yourself in the foot! Also, beware of establishing too many affiliate relationships. When people click through a link, many of them will not return to the source. Although commissions are nice to have, you don't want to create a mass exodus of potential customers to other sites. Your main focus is still on selling your *own* products, not somebody else's.

On the other hand, always allow other companies to link to *you* as much as they want. If they ask for a small commission, pay it. Traffic that hits your store as the result of an offsite link is virtually always composed of new customers; even if the visitors aren't actually new, they probably would *not* have visited your site that day without the link. Therefore, any purchases they make are pure gold—you haven't lost anything. Commissions, therefore, are almost always worth it. So feel free to encourage other companies to get on board! As you grow more popular, you will begin to get more offers, which will in turn generate higher sales. Affiliate programs are an excellent opportunity—seek out interested companies, and always take advantage of those that seek you.

Before you make the decision to partner with another company, however, you'll need to take a few precautionary steps in order to protect your own business. Just as savvy customers examine your credentials and testimonials before making a purchase, so your company should test the reputation of any business that wants to team up. Don't be taken in by either a fraudulent or unreliable company. Once you have formed a business relationship, their actions will reflect on you—so take this step very seriously. Your own image is at stake. Be sure to perform a few background checks in advance.

- **Use Search Engines.** There's absolutely no excuse not to perform this check; it's ridiculously easy, and absolutely free. Run the company name through a search engine and see what it drags up. At the most basic level, you just want to make sure that it actually exists! Other than that, you want to dig deeper to see what kind of reputation it has. You do not want to associate with a company that could sully your good name.

- **Use the U.S. Postal Service.** If this company is genuine, it should have a physical mailing address. A business may be able to fake an online storefront, but it's a lot more difficult to fake an actual geographic location. Visit the U.S. Postal Service homepage, and verify the address with which the partner company has provided you. Once there, head over to the ZIP code look-up feature, which allows you to enter any given address. It will then print out the name of the company housed at that location. If there are any problems, the function should notify you of that as well.

- **Talk to Past and Present Clients.** Talk to the individuals and companies whom your affiliate company has served. See if they have generally been happy with the quality of service provided them—and if not, ask why. This procedure may be costly in terms of time, but it is also incredibly accurate.

- **Talk to Other Associates.** Interview the current associates of the other company. Again, these are the people who know your potential partner the best. Ask them to be as specific as possible about their likes and dislikes.

Once you have assured yourself of the affiliate's qualifications and background, it's time to put the partnership in writing: Whatever agreement you reach, always draw up a formal contract. Although it's easier to settle an affiliate deal on a "handshake," such casual relationships can lay the groundwork for future problems. Be sure to define the exact parameters of the agreement: the flat fee or percentage of each commission, the rights and responsibilities of each participant, and the length of time for which the contract is valid. The Web often suggests a deceptively relaxed atmosphere; don't be lulled into complacency. Always obtain legal protection, just as your company would in offline contracts. It could save you a great deal of both money and frustration.

Giveaways

Giveaway programs are a great way to lure in new visitors. People are a lot more willing to try something new if they receive something free in return. When you display your banner ads, you need to offer a compelling reason for the surfer to drop everything and head your way. There are several different ways to accomplish this, but the most popular method is to mention a "freebie." People love free stuff—they'll even change their shopping patterns in order to take advantage of a good deal.

Free shipping is usually the most effective offer, since the shipping charge is one of the main drawbacks to shopping online. It also has universal appeal—everybody loves free shipping! If you remove that obstacle, people are a lot more willing to commit to a purchase. In addition, it's easy for you to handle, because this particular freebie does not affect your inventory. (You'll never run out of "free shipping" due to demand!)

> Giveaways are a great opportunity to get rid of overstock!

Other than shipping, you can give away various sundry items that might be of interest to customers. If you are having trouble liquidating overstocked merchandise, you can use that as your freebie. Just be careful about how you market the giveaway—never make any promises that you can't back up. A truly inferior product or tacky merchandise will disenchant customers who were expecting a nice gift. Also make sure that you have enough product. Always overestimate the amount you'll probably need. If you sell out before you can fulfill customer demand, they probably won't come back to your site. It's never good to start a business relationship with a broken promise.

Freebies are the most effective when you only offer them to new customers. It's too expensive to offer everybody free shipping at every visit. In addition, you'll lose a considerable amount of money if every customer receives a gift. The purpose behind a giveaway is to recruit new customers, to coax them to shop at your store. Established customers have already been coaxed! There are other, less expensive ways to keep them happy. They can take advantage of frequent-buyer programs.

Frequent-Buyer Programs

Customers are far more powerful on the Internet than they are offline. You *must* provide tangible incentives for them to shop at your store—or they'll go elsewhere.

Customer loyalty is a life-and-death issue for most online stores. In an Internet market, it's incredibly easy for customers to visit a different store each time they log on. And they do—there are no physical restraints that cause them to patronize the same corner grocery store for twenty years. Since proximity is no longer an important factor for most surfers, they're free to "shop around" in countless stores before they settle on a favorite. The scary truth is that when people pop up at your site, they'll probably never return. The goal, therefore, is to increase the "stickiness" of your store. In other words, you should create the kind of environment that encourages repeat business. Provide compelling reasons for customers to choose you over your competitors. If you don't, they'll continue to bounce around until somebody *else* wins their permanent affections. Incredibly, a Jupiter Communications report notes that about 75 percent of online consumers participate in customer-loyalty programs—that's a high percentage. Advertising does not simply exist to attract new customers; it also helps to maintain the ones you already have.

Although many bricks-and-mortar companies have never needed to give away free stuff, the Internet market is changing all the rules. Whether or not you have a loyal real-life clientele, you should be establishing customer retention programs for the online store. One way for you to do this is to create frequent-buyer programs. Offer goodies to customers who meet certain advertised requirements: discounts, free products, free shipping, or anything else that might provide an incentive to make repeat visits to your store. People are much more likely to keep coming back if they know that on the tenth purchase, they'll get a ten-dollar rebate off the receipt total. Just make sure that you clearly advertise your policy—a frequent buyer program won't affect shoppers if they don't even know it exists!

So what's the difference between gifts for new customers and a frequent-buyer program? Well, each category has pros and cons. New customers receive a prize just for showing up; loyal customers have to *earn* the freebies. On the other hand, for new customers the giveaway is a onetime thing, while the regular clientele can earn an unlimited number of discounts or free stuff. When employed in concert, giveaways and loyalty programs are incredibly effective.

Frequent-buyer programs are also an excellent way to encourage customers to fill out personal information forms. If they know that registration will make them eligible for an attractive offer, they'll be far happier to enter their name, address, and other statistical data. It also offers the aura of exclusivity, rather like joining a club. Try posting a graphic that proclaims the offer. If you run a store named Shoebox Shoes, fly a big ad: "Get Free ShoeBucks! Click here to learn more." Once the shopper clicks through the ad, explain your policy and ask them to fill out a simple form to become a "preferred shopper." Now they can earn their way towards store credit on all merchandise!

Although it may not be fun for your company to give away free stuff, the nature of e-commerce has nearly made it a requirement: A Society of Consumer Affairs Professionals (SOCAP) report notes that a whopping 96 percent of online shoppers believe that sales and rebates are "important" at e-tail sites. In order to be competitive, you need to edge out your rivals—and to do that, you must win the hearts of the public. The resulting increase in overall traffic should more than pay for any losses you incur from the various promotions.

Contests

Contests are fun for customers. They're also a great way for you to coax customers into giving personal data!

On a related note, holding a contest is a great way to attract traffic from new and old visitors alike. It's also much easier for your company to arrange, since there is a strictly limited number of winners—most usually, just one. And, because you'll only need to arrange for one prize, you can invest in a much nicer gift. Depending on your company and its balance sheet, you can give away any number of things: expensive products, mini vacations, free services, cash, or just about anything else that might interest your customers. If the prize package is attractive enough, you might attract a considerable number of participants, some of whom will probably make purchases once they arrive. Contests are a valuable tool. They bribe new people into visiting without penalizing the longtime customer—and they're infrequent enough to be less burdensome for the average small company.

Gift Reminders

Offering gift reminders is a great idea if you sell merchandise that falls into the normal categories: flowers, candies, toys, clothes, power tools, books, or any other items that might possibly be given as presents. On a popular page, preferably the homepage, post a prominent graphic that encourages shoppers to "Sign Up For Our Free Gift Reminder Service!" Once they have clicked through, have the visitor fill out a brief form. It should clearly outline your service policy, explaining what it involves. So what *should* it involve? Usually, you just store the pertinent names and/or dates provided by the customer, then send her a brief e-mail reminder one week or so in advance. Customers love this service; they no longer have to worry about forgetting a friend's or relative's birthday, anniversary, retirement, or whatever! (That's assuming, of course, that they check their e-mail at frequent intervals.) Gift reminders means happier customers.

So what's in it for you? In the first place, it's a soft-handed method of encouraging customers to spend more money at your store. If they receive the reminder from you, they are more likely to stop at your store *first* when shopping for that very gift. Never underestimate the power of suggestion! Even if they don't wind up buying anything from your business at that time, the service still helps keep your name foremost in their minds. In other words, you won't become just another long-forgotten, generic online store. The service can help to build your overall traffic and sales, and it costs you virtually nothing. But aside from sales promotion, gift reminders are also another great opportunity to get visitors to divulge some personal data for your records! You'll have to request basic information such as name and e-mail address, but you can also include a few other non-threatening categories. Include a checkbox asking them if they would like to be included on your mailing list. Since the visitor is applying for a free service, he is likely to be willing to spend a *little* extra time filling out a survey. Just remember to keep it brief—if you abuse the customers' patience, they might leave the site!

After the visitors have completed the form, transfer them to a thank-you screen. Let them know that they should shortly be receiving a confirmation e-mail from your company; then send it within twenty-four hours. The e-mail should include another summary of the policy and another thank-you, just for the sake of reinforcement.

Creating a Community

Don't just run an impersonal store. Create a fun, social atmosphere by hosting a community!

One of the best ways to generate customer loyalty is to foster a virtual community. Virtual communities are still a fairly new form of social interaction, but they can be a powerful force. They usually develop around a common personal trait; some communities are centered around a demographic profile, others around a shared interest or goal. There are currently many thriving groups for women, seniors, specific ethnicities, religions, and so on—but since you run a store, you'll probably want to focus on a hobby or interest specific to your business. Gardening supply stores and nurseries can support a horticulture club, for example; music stores can host guitar discussion groups. The purpose is to allow potential customers to bond with one another—and with the sponsor, your store.

Internet communities can strengthen lasting relationships, providing people with a place to share their interest with like-minded individuals. Such groups are especially helpful for the more obscure pursuits. People who have a passion for an uncommon hobby may find it difficult to meet other enthusiasts in a real-life setting. Virtual communities allow geographically far-flung individuals to socialize in a low-pressure setting, and without having to pay a cent. Suddenly, the amateur potter can discuss tips and techniques with other people who enjoy the art. It's all about *connection*. What with telecommuting and increasingly hectic work schedules, our computerized present has a tendency to isolate people from one another. It's nice to know that other technologies can help dissolve those same barriers.

Your company can create a virtual community in several different ways. Some are almost self-supporting; others require a high level of maintenance, but the payoff can be especially rewarding.

- **Discussion or Message Boards.** Discussion boards are the easiest form of community to sustain. Any member can "post" a message on the board, where it is exhibited for public viewing. People can read and respond to the message right on your Web site, or even respond to other responses, thus creating limited "discussions" over a period of minutes or even days. Since they don't occur in real time, there's no need to support a constant presence, which is easy on your company. If you develop enough traffic, you can even create more than one board: One can be devoted to talking "shop," while another can center around personal topics. In this way, visitors can participate only in a focused group if they so desire, but they can also get to know one another better. Personal topic boards can really help cement friendships and create a lasting virtual community. If it's successful enough, people will visit every day just to chat with one another—and you'll have become a desirable destination location!

    Still, you'll want to establish some definite ground rules. Discussion boards can become out of control if they lack a moderating presence. Ask that all customers restrict themselves to pertinent material—although you might want to allow personal exchanges, you'll still want to ban offensive material. Some people are simply rude, other mischievous surfers will visit random boards and try to stir up fights just for the entertainment value. (When they purposefully incite inexperienced chatters, it's called "trolling for newbies.")

Before anyone is allowed to post anything, you should require him to fill out a brief form, including his name and e-mail address. To double-check the identity, you can then e-mail a password to the account he has provided. This part should ideally be computer-generated, so that the visitor can begin participating immediately. If you lack the resources to generate automatic responses, at least make sure that you respond to the request within twenty-four hours, in order to shorten the waiting period. In this manner, you can keep a close eye on who gets to post on the board. Although visitors are still allowed to publicly post under any name, even anonymously, your program will know which e-mail address generated the message. If someone abuses the privilege, you can easily "ban" her by invalidating her password.

....

Make sure that you control access to the discussion board.
Keep everyone civil.

....

Some companies and communities add one more precaution: They don't allow people to use free e-mail accounts—such as Hotmail—to post, since people can so easily obtain them. In other words, if you banned someone, he wouldn't be able to just get a new free account, reapply and cause more trouble under a different name. Yet since this is a real inconvenience for many people with free accounts—almost all of whom are "law-abiding"—you might want to avoid imposing this restriction unless it becomes necessary.

Despite your best efforts, a few problems are bound to

arise, but that's not a big problem. If off-topic comments and rude messages (the latter also known as "flames") make their way onto the board, just have the moderator pull them as soon as possible. Because of the necessary monitoring, you'll want a qualified employee to visit the board once or twice each day to keep them on track.

In actuality, you don't have to start your own discussion group in order to take advantage of the method—you can be a member of someone else's. You or a knowledgeable employee can personally join discussion lists in order to create a little name recognition for your company. If you have a valid or informative point to make, you can feel free to express yourself eloquently and then sign the mini article with your company's name and contact information. If other members are sufficiently impressed with your grasp of the topic, they may decide to wander over and check it out for themselves. And, hey—if they like what they see and spread the word, you've created a little free buzz for your online store.

Just remember to adhere to standard Internet etiquette. Discussion groups, forums, and message boards are not supposed to serve as a personal soapbox from which to preach your sales gospel. People will be offended if you engage in blatant advertising, and they might boycott your store. Some businesspeople try a more subtle approach. They create a good topical article and then post it with a large number of discussion or newsgroups. Such an activity is called "cross-posting." They figure that they can cover a lot of ground with one document. Unfortunately, this too can backfire if a surfer finds out about the repeat posts. Such action is seen as a breach of good manners, and is called excessive cross-posting, or ECP.

Incidentally, Internet slang truly is an interesting mix of terms, especially in this area. ECP is sometimes referred to as velveeta. But it doesn't end there: If your company mixes the unsolicited e-mail habit with ECP, then your marketing strategies are known as neither spam nor velveeta. Instead, surfers call this specific combination of offenses "jello." Go figure!

•   **Newsgroups.** Newsgroups are, essentially, giant public message boards. They are hosted by large corporate or private news servers, which are in turn governed by a system called the Usenet. As a rule, they are almost always confined to a specific topic or interest, are supposed to be more informative than opinion-based, and are limited to subscribers. But that's pretty much where the restrictions end. In the first place, the news servers usually have no personal interest in the group; the servers mostly operate according to a rather laissez-faire doctrine. In addition to this lack of absolute authority, virtually anyone can start a newsgroup, and anyone can join. Such loose standards have ensured that these ostensibly dry newsgroups can be quite chaotic!

    Web site message boards are usually kept under the tight watch of a moderator; most newsgroups are more like the Internet's "wild, wild west." Since it's almost impossible to get kicked off of a newsgroup, many entrepreneurs have found them an easy advertising venue. They are lulled into a sense of security by the "newsy" aura of the group, and begin to think that their own ads qualify as news, too. They might then write a promotional page thinly disguised as an article, and post it on a newsgroup of related interest. This is a definite mistake. If a businessperson oversteps the bounds of a message board, she'll merely have her access revoked. Newsgroup justice is radically different. Since no one's in charge, posters often resort to playing the role of cyberspace vigilantes. If participants begin to suspect you of gross self-promotion, you just might find your own e-mail address overloaded with retaliatory spam or hit with an e-mail bomb. Such tactics can easily cause your system to "overheat" and crash, so be wary of raising too many Usenet hackles.

The best approach to newsgroup publicity is to use the same low-profile techniques as you would with a discussion group. First wander the news servers to find the newsgroups that best relate to your own company. Do a lot of "lurking," or visit the site without actually participating. Get a feel for the unique atmosphere of the group before you try anything. Once you feel comfortable, write a good quality article that makes an interesting point but says nothing about your company. When you sign it, include a few short lines of contact info beneath your name. And never, ever cross-post. Velveeta (see "Discussion or Message Boards") is almost as hated as spam. Let the other readers come to you—if they're interested, they can figure out how to contact you on their own. Don't push.

- **Chat Groups.** Chat groups are powerful tools, but they also require a great deal of work on your part. In the first place, the communication is in real time, so you'll need to appoint someone to monitor the chat room on a more consistent basis. Your company may or may not decide to integrate the regular chat room with a tech support service to conserve resources; the moderator could fulfill both the regulating and troubleshooting capacities. Well-managed chat rooms can be a real attraction for the general public. You can schedule specific hours each week to be devoted to a single topic. Interested people can then show up at the appointed time to either participate or just enjoy lurking.

  In addition to supporting routine discussions, your marketing department can work to host guest speakers, or experts in a relevant field. As with written testimonials, many qualified individuals are willing to help out for free, since the discussion is such good publicity for their own company or field. With a little advertising savvy, you can notify both your new and regular customers of upcoming sessions, so that people can show up particularly to hear out a certain speaker or topic. Your company can essentially "sell" access to information; even though the discussions are free, the growth in both your potential and actual customer bases can be tremendous. Just remember that whatever you do, be sure to keep a tight rein on the ongoing discussions. If a few members begin to insult one another, the chat can quickly degenerate into a flame session—and once people become disgusted enough to leave, they will likely never come back.

E-Mail Marketing Strategies

E-mail is cheap, effective, *and* incredibly versatile!

E-mail is probably the cheapest form of active marketing your company can initiate. The online advertising forms we've discussed up to this point are fairly passive; they are merely placed in the path of normal customer traffic in the hope that they'll attract customers. E-mail, on the other hand, is an incredibly effective way of reaching out to the customers yourself. Instead of having to wait for visitors to seek *you*, you can recruit your own business—and all at a minimum cost. Nevertheless, there is a big catch: You *must not* abuse e-mail marketing strategies, or your company will run into incredible opposition—of the social and perhaps even legal kind. In fact, before we discuss the most effective uses of e-mail, it would probably be prudent to directly address this hot-button issue.

E-mail marketing at its simplest is simply sending advertising and news tidbits to interested customers. The key word, of course, is *interested*. The generation of unsolicited mass e-mails, known colloquially as "spamming," constitutes a significant breach of cyberspace manners. Although it can be effective, it has the power to irritate like no other form of advertising.

Some companies feel that spam should be no more offensive

than normal junk mail or telemarketing. There is logic to the sentiment, especially considering that all three activities operate on the same principle: If you blitz enough consumers with your sales pitch, you're guaranteed at least a small return of interest. Yet strangely, although junk mail and telemarketing undeniably annoy many people, they have never provoked as violent a reaction as spam. So what's the difference? It probably has something to do with the physical limitations of the traditional methods.

When a company sends notification that you're a "finalist" in a contest you've never entered, you probably throw it out. Likewise, other sales and unwanted catalogs also usually make the quick trip from mailbox to garbage can; you keep what you want and toss what you don't. Sometimes the ads can be annoying, but most people don't feel the need to make an official protest. After all, it's only a few items per day at most. Yet what if the volume and frequency of unsolicited mail increased exponentially? Imagine that hundreds of companies sent mass mailings nearly every day, to the point where it became difficult to find your bills and letters among the gigantic mounds of ads and flyers. It's likely that your patience would dissolve within days—such a deluge of material could be construed as an invasion of privacy.

Granted, such an event will probably never happen. Why? Because it's time-consuming for companies to arrange mailings, and it would require the use of a gargantuan amount of paper; running such a giant campaign would be prohibitively expensive. In other words, the physical limitations of the medium prevent businesses from abusing the right to send unsolicited print ads. But e-mail is a different story. You don't need to purchase supplies to create mass mailings, nor do you need to stuff the envelopes or truck them out to the post office. It's very easy to write one brief form letter or flyer and then import a mailing list to the address line. After that, all you need to do is click "Send." Technically speaking, thousands of companies can spam millions of people—and they can do it for free. E-mail, therefore, inherently poses a far greater risk to consumers than does the traditional mail system. Web surfers do not want to log on to their account only to find two thousand new messages, only three of which are of legitimate interest to the user. Believe it or not, such things do happen. Spam realistically threatens the privacy of the average consumer—that's the main reason people are campaigning so forcefully against it.

....

Never use e-mail to attract new customers.

....

E-mail is a powerful tool, but it must be employed in a responsible manner. In almost all cases, this means obtaining the advance permission of recipients. Never market to people who were not offered the choice to "opt out" of your mailing list. Small virtual companies often see e-mail as an unparalleled opportunity to reach new customers. Don't succumb to the temptation! E-mail should be reserved for established, interested clients. There are plenty of other, less intrusive ways to generate new traffic.

So, dire warnings aside, what's the best way to avoid being accused of spamming? Wage an effective campaign to prompt customers to *ask* for material! On your homepage and throughout your site, be sure to invite customers to "Join Our Mailing List." You can also allow customers the chance to "opt in" at the point of purchase: When they provide their e-mail addresses, have two radio buttons that let the customers choose to either receive messages from your company or remain ad-free. Once they have indicated their consent, you have free rein to market to your heart's content. It's still not a good idea to produce an obnoxious amount of material, but at least the customers on *this* list have given their official sanction.

The good news is that since you're already an established business, you won't have to worry excessively about reaching "critical mass," that point at which an Internet venture becomes viable. Start-up companies must begin with nothing—no publicity, no experience, and no customers. The first few weeks or months can be a true challenge; it's hard to survive that initial stage. After all, they have to attract all new customers, people who have no shared history with the company or any level of trust. Your business, on the other hand, already has a solid foundation on which to base your efforts, which includes an existing clientele. Therefore, getting a start in e-mail marketing shouldn't be much of a problem—the only worries are about which strategies to employ!

- **Building Your Own List.** The most reputable way to develop a marketing list is to build it yourself. In other words, you and your employees handpick and assemble the entire thing. This has the advantage of ensuring that you know something about the customer—it also helps you maintain an air of legitimacy. So how do you build up a solid mailing list?

    Some companies are proactive, and aggressively search for new names. They try to avoid the "spammer" label by combing the Internet personally, to choose individuals who might be interested in their products. Among other things, they poke around in related-interest Web sites, checking out the discussion groups to see who looks promising. All available data on each likely candidate is then saved and catalogued. On a periodic basis, employees mail a brief, personalized note to the prospective customers, inviting them to the Web site. Is this ethical? That has yet to be decided. The involved companies believe that only automated mass mailings qualify as spam. Therefore, since their method involves a large investment of time on their part, they argue that the resulting campaign should be no more offensive than a telemarketer pitch.

    Still, despite such compromise tactics the controversy rages on—many people have since argued that regardless of technique, unsolicited messages are still a nuisance. Our advice is to avoid contacting customers without some form of prior permission. You don't need the hassle, and you can live without it. Usually, businesses only resort to such aggressive tactics because they desperately need to build a clientele—and fast. Startups are under tremendous pressure to reach critical mass if they want to survive. Your company, however, does not depend on its online purchasing site for survival. Although your online "store" will probably start out by netting you only a small percentage of total customers, that's okay. Your bricks-and-mortar store should remain profitable, so an initial scarcity of online customers won't put you out of business. So don't worry—you've got a safety net!

It's better to be safe than sorry: As a rule of thumb, never e-mail customers unless they have already given their permission.

Another active way to add to your mailing list is to rent the addresses of customers who have pre-approved the reception of e-mails on a particular subject of interest. Believe it or not, there are actually companies that earn a living just compiling a database of people who are interested in receiving e-mail ads. Legitimate companies of this type include only those people who opt in to the program, and they should provide ways to quit the list as well. They then make their money by allowing online e-tailers and other companies to use the lists for marketing purposes. The beauty of the arrangement is that you can reap the benefits of a huge customer list without offending any of the recipients. You can also launch a huge publicity campaign in a matter of hours, instead of the weeks necessary to design and mass-mail a print ad. In addition, these companies will generally arrange the list in topical subcategories, so that you can reach only those customers who are likely to be interested in your particular offer. You can generate a good deal of immediate traffic when this tactic is used judiciously.

A few words of warning, however: Be sure that the company you contact is reputable. Some smaller businesses will engage in unethical practices, either by selling their private lists without the consent of the customers, or by including people who have no connection with that company whatsoever. Take this matter seriously; if you employ the services of a shady business, you'll be found guilty by association. Beware of deals that are too good to be true, since they usually are. Law-abiding companies will normally charge you for a one- or two-time use of the list, and they will want to mail the ad from their own personal server in order to control access to their databases. You can also expect to pay a few hundred dollars for the privilege— most list companies charge ten to twenty cents for each name. The best tactic is simply to work only with large, well-known portals such as Yahoo! that rent lists as a side business, or big rental companies like PostMaster Direct Response. Because they rely on a good reputation for their livelihood, they have a vested interest in keeping business dealings on the up-and-up.

• **Letting the List Build Itself.** Because the aggressive pursuit of addresses can prove such a thorny issue, many experts suggest that you use such tactics only when necessary. Start-ups might indeed need the initial blitzkrieg campaign to achieve profitability, but that's not necessarily true for you. Since you already have a good customer base, you should probably stick mostly to the more passive methods. This means letting your own customers volunteer for your personal list. It may be smaller, but it will be both well-targeted and gathered in a manner that is above reproach.

So how do you do it? As mentioned previously, just publicize the service on your site and let the customers come to you. Your salespeople in the bricks-and-mortar store can also suggest the mailing list to walk-in customers. If you promote the service in a nonthreatening manner, people are more willing to give it a try. Also, be sure to emphasize the benefits when you ask. Which statement is more likely to get results?

- "Do you mind if we put you on our mailing list?"
- "Would you like us to send you some free information about upcoming sales?"

The first sentence makes the service seem like a burden. Customers will immediately think of junk mail and spam. The second option casts the mailing list as helpful, as a free service that the customer might enjoy. People are far more likely to respond favorably to the second sentence. Just be extremely careful not to abuse their trust in *any* way—never inundate customers with ads, and never, ever rent or sell your own list to other businesses. No matter how much they offer to pay you, you'll still lose out when word leaks that your company is untrustworthy.

Be sure to preserve your customers' anonymity when you send mass e-mails.

So how do you design a quality e-mail ad? Just take the normal content guidelines for the Internet and extend them to the new venue. In the first place, you'll want to safeguard the privacy of your customers. Whenever you issue a mass e-mailing, never publicly expose your mailing list by placing the addresses in the "To" or "CC" fields of the message. Each recipient would be able to see everyone else's address—and that's obviously a big no-no. Instead, use the "BCC" field; this stands for "*blind* carbon copy," which means that the list will not be visible to addressees. In the "To" field, you can always place your company's own address.

Your e-mails should also be as direct as possible. When you're trying to sell somebody a product or service, you should get right to the point. After all, aren't you annoyed by salespeople who ramble? Be direct, and state clearly what the offer involves. This includes creating an unambiguous message for the subject line, so that the customer knows immediately whether or not she's interested. A more exciting, misleading subject might entice more customers to open the e-mail, but they'll probably be irritated upon realizing the deception. In that case, they'll either begin ignoring your messages altogether or remove themselves from the mailing list—and that's certainly not the path to success. Don't alienate your customers. Honesty is truly the best policy.

Next, make sure that the ad is well-written. Remember that the ease and speed of e-mail often lulls companies into a certain carelessness of manner. Don't fall into this trap. Even electronic ads have a strong effect on the image of your business. If the material is badly composed and sloppily edited, you will probably lose business.

Keep your e-mails simple. Leave out the fireworks and let the text do the talking!

You should also leave out the bells and whistles. Simplicity is even more important on e-mail than on the general Web site, since customers are more likely to have plug-ins for ordinary surfing. E-mail programs are liable to be pretty basic, in which case your fabulous HTML message complete with banner graphic will be opened as a series of meaningless code characters. Not only is this useless to the customer, but it's also incredibly annoying. Leave off attachments, too, unless the shopper specifically requests material that can best be provided in this form. In that case, make sure that he knows about the impending message, lest he suspect it of being a virus. Lots of Web savvy people delete all e-mails with attachments unless they come from someone they know personally. What good is your ad if people kill it on sight?

Traditional e-mail marketing—if the word "traditional" is permissible—revolves around the sending of mass advertisements. Normal ads are great, but they still have drawbacks. Even if the customer requests mailings from your company, they can still be a bit heavy-handed for the average person's taste. Sales and other promotional messages should not be sent more than a few times each month, or the customer will quickly tire of them. There's a fine line between aggressive promotion and overkill! Fortunately, in the past couple of years, companies have been coming up with alternative ways to promote themselves—strategies that are far subtler and more effective than the standard method.

- **Discussion Lists.** One option is for your company to sponsor a discussion list. Discussion lists are like the e-mail equivalent of a group seminar. A moderator is appointed to maintain the peace and ensure that the exchanges remain topical, and she usually kicks off the forum by posing a provocative question or comment. The message is sent to all involved participants, who can then add their own opinions to the discussion. Everyone involved can read everyone else's contribution, which can make for a very lively experience. The moderator controls all "flames" and makes sure that disagreements don't become too personal. Unlike message boards, discussion lists will be sent to the members on a regular basis. It's a nice way for you to maintain public interest in your company, because the public is reminded of it. With message or discussion boards, visitors have to actively seek your site—not so with discussion lists. Once they join, you can initiate discussion.

  When done properly, discussion groups are a great way to entertain people and keep them interested in a particular subject. Such groups also offer the participants a feeling of involvement—getting feedback from one's peers can be incredibly rewarding. All these qualities contribute to the community feeling generated in relation to your site. If people begin associating your name with an enjoyable discussion list, traffic at your site will probably increase. Participants will start visiting for reasons other than just to make a purchase, and once they arrive they might wind up spending a little money. Even if they don't, at least you might prevent them from patronizing one of your competitors when they *do* buy something. If you become a destination location, your sales will skyrocket. Even better, companies such as eGroups.com will provide you with free services to help you support group communication.

- **Electronic Magazines.** Electronic magazines, also known as e-zines or zines, are basically just newsy e-mails that aim to inform rather than sell. Customers will be a lot more likely to eagerly anticipate mailings from your company if they come in the palatable form of articles, updates, factoids, and other little tidbits regarding their own subjects of interest. How often have we all sorted the day's mail, then tossed the ads to the side while we grab the latest magazine and head off to the couch? E-zines make it possible for your company to avoid the bad rep of other, pushier corporations.

  If your business sells power tools, you can produce a virtual magazine that involves carpentry projects or how-to home repairs. You might include interviews with various experts in woodworking—maybe someone who's going to be the next Bob Vila! It doesn't have to be incredibly sophisticated, as long as your target audience will find it interesting. Yet make sure that it's well-written and structured; just like your Web site, an e-magazine represents your company. A half-hearted attempt will reflect poorly on you and might very well *lose* your company customers, rather than attract them.

  It's also important to implement and stick to a normal "publishing" schedule. Many e-zines are monthlies, but if you can handle the workload, try issuing a new edition each week. The product does not need to be incredibly complicated; usually one main article or interview with a few other factoids will suffice. Companies such as e-Journal and ListCity actually make registered e-zines available to the general public; if you need advice on format or content, you can check out their Web sites and read a few samples. Who knows—if it becomes popular, you might want to register your own publication! Archiving the e-zine can be a great publicity maneuver, provided that it's a quality work. Subscription would no longer be limited to your current clientele; readers who like your e-zine, despite having never heard of your site, might become interested enough to stop by for a visit. They might even become loyal customers. Just know that whatever you do, stay on schedule. People can become as irate about tardy e-zines as they do about a late newspaper!

Think of e-magazines as "stealth" advertising!

E-magazines are a powerful tool, largely because they're subtle. Customers will perceive such publications more as entertainment and read them happily; they won't feel assaulted or exploited, as they might if you overuse your e-mail advertisements. Yet at the same time, the shoppers' interest in the hobby or field is kept at a high level, and they are more likely to return to your site on a regular basis. Indeed, when used properly, e-magazines are every bit as effective as traditional marketing methods. They're also fun, and have a softer touch than almost all other forms of advertising.

Creating and Promoting Good Links

Customers appreciate Web sites that have good quality links.

A great way to improve the public image of your store is to associate yourself with other, more established companies. You can do this easily and free of charge, merely by providing links to any Web site you desire. This technique is especially simple because you don't need the permission of other sites in order to rub elbows with them—in fact, they're usually quite happy if you do establish a link, since that helps to boost their own traffic. Remember that some Web companies will even link to your homepage in return for the "favor"—that, or pay a commission for each sale that originates from your link. What do you get in return? Fortuately, the expression "guilt by association" can work for successes, too. When you list the names of reputable companies on your site, you're subtly placing yourself among the more esteemed ranks.

The addition of links can also promote the image of your store as a destination location. It promotes a relaxed environment, one in which your company seems willing to share its resources with customers. If you create a clever enough set of links, visitors might start visiting your site just for the sake of convenience; after all, if you post related companies all on one page, your customers won't have to surf around as much. The more people you attract, even if they don't normally purchase anything from you, the better your stock with advertising companies. If you can build a solid amount of traffic, you'll even be able to command a decent price for other companies' banners.

There are a few problems that might arise from the use of external links, some of which have been touched on previously. Remember not to overdo the number of links on the site, or you'll encourage a customer stampede to the nearest exit. Also, don't link to your direct competitors, unless you have a special arrangement with the other company. (For instance, if they're willing to reciprocate with a link to your site, you might consider striking a deal.) After all, advertising for your competition is tantamount to handing customers a one-way ticket out of your online store. Don't do it! Links simply work best when they lead to companies that are only *tangentially* related to yours.

Do your homework. Research all potential links.

You should also carefully research the businesses for which you provide links, because listing the name of another company on your site is a tacit endorsement. Make *very* sure that this endorsement is justified, or you'll wind up in the embarrassing position of having led customers to a disreputable company. If someone has a bad experience in a store they reached through your link, they might very well place some of the blame on your doorstep. It might not be your fault, but actual guilt is irrelevant when you're losing customers left and right. Play it safe, and do your homework.

Awards

If you feel particularly confident about the quality of your Web site, then you might want to consider the advertising potential of an award. Strangely enough, it does qualify as a form of advertising; being officially recognized by a different, respected Internet site is obviously a great boost for your business. An award essentially helps market your company for you; when Web companies bestow any type of honor, they virtually always post the winner on their own sites. You thus benefit in two different ways: Not only do you receive the wholehearted recommendation of another business, but you also get to advertise the distinction on your own Web site!

> Winning an award can do wonders for your public image.

The recommendation is probably the most helpful, since it brings you new traffic. Many consumers will try a new site when they hear positive reviews about it elsewhere—it's cyberspace word of mouth! Some of them will even return to the award host site on a weekly or monthly basis to see what new suggestions it posts. In general, you'll receive a good influx of visitors who are truly interested in your products, and have chosen your store since it won an award.

You'll also attract a few curious individuals who are merely interested in seeing why the site won—they might not buy anything, but if sufficiently impressed they can help generate buzz. In addition, if you have generated a groundbreaking design or service, you'll get attention from the ever-valuable tech crowd.

Awards are also nice trophies to flaunt in your own cyber living room. Remember that your company's image is extremely important when you're trying to sell goods over the Internet. The customers are a great deal more cautious about making purchases, since they know that online appearances can be very deceiving. An award can go a long way towards encouraging tentative shoppers to become loyal customers; the honor conveys a certain prestige along with a presumed guarantee of quality, so surfers feel more comfortable trusting your business to follow through on its obligations. Since many people do not know about the existence of digital certificates, so an award is like a highly visible substitute. In addition, the "lemming mentality" makes a certain contribution: "If everybody else likes this store, then I'll shop here too." The greater part of the public prefers to follow rather than lead—if you can convince the leaders that your site is worth taking a look at, then others will follow.

Naturally, there's a gigantic limitation on this form of advertising; getting an award is not exactly within your control. You can't force anyone to visit, much less recommend your site, so you might not have any awards to speak of for a long time after you go online—if ever. Still, you should know to properly exploit the honor should it be granted to you. In other words, make sure that people actually know about it! Revisit the search directories and change your business description to include a mention of the award; also, take the time to post it prominently on the homepage of your Web site. It won't do you any good if your visitors are not aware that you've won anything. You can also increase the likelihood of an award by nominating yourself at Web sites that allow suggestions. Look around at

Web sites that relate to your business, and see if one or more of them grant awards. If you put your company's site forward as a candidate, at least they'll know to consider you. In addition, if you win, then the award will be exhibited to a receptive audience. Many search engines, such as Lycos and Yahoo, also give awards, so you'll want to check them out and see what their rules and regulations are. Getting promoted by a portal can create an unbelievable amount of business for any e-tailer. If you are recognized by a major company, just be prepared to handle a sudden increase in traffic. Make sure you have the necessary bandwidth!

Take the initiative—create and grant your own award!

Awards can also be useful in other ways. They can benefit the host company as well as the recipient—which is, of course, largely why companies grant awards in the first place. If your site generates a decent amount of traffic, then you might be interested in hosting your *own* award or awards. The simple act of passing favorable judgment on other companies reflects well on your cyberspace stature; your company will seem more respectable, its image more professional. If the process becomes popular enough, some people will also start increasing the frequency of their visits to see whom you might pick next. The increase in traffic then both adds to your sales *and* lets you ask a higher price from companies who wish to place banner ads on your site.

So how do you "invent" an award? It's easy enough. Simply choose a site each week or month that exhibits excellence in a particular way, and post their company name on your site. Give the honor a clear, brief title. Also, select qualifying criteria that pertain to your type of business—albeit indirectly. In order for the award to seem reasonable, it has to relate to your company in some way; however, you don't want to advertise the merit of a direct competitor! For example, if you run a clothing store, you can create an award for the best fashion-related Web site that week. Regardless of how you handle the issue, if you do decide to create an award, first make certain that your own site is good enough to be taken seriously.

Saying Thanks

For countless generations, mothers have impressed upon their children the importance of writing thank-you notes. Take a page from their book: Appreciate your customers. It's easy to give excellent customer service in your bricks-and-mortar store—you can smile, chat with the shoppers, perhaps take the extra time to help them find what they want. Yet cyberspace, for all its benefits and customization, lacks the warmth of human interaction. When you can't personally visit with your customers, it's all too easy to lose the easy rapport that makes for a loyal clientele. Don't let it happen!

Some of the most important ingredients in an online store are in the details. Since shopping online can feel impersonal, do everything in your power to establish a relationship with your customers. This includes writing thank-you notes—and automated confirmation messages after an online purchase do not qualify! Although it might be too troublesome to thank shoppers after every purchase, take the time to send a note to your best customers from time to time. Briefly and sincerely express your appreciation for their business, then offer them a small discount or gift. Such an unexpected note is the kind of gesture that makes for a fiercely loyal clientele—and thus Internet success.

Glossary

24 × 7 A reference to any company or service that runs twenty-four hours a day, seven days a week.

access provider The company or service that provides paying customers with Internet access; not to be confused with an ISP, which provides Internet *service*. See also **ISP**.

acquirer Internet slang for a bank that provides online merchant services.

affiliate Any company with which your business has a professional relationship. The association usually stems from an agreement to exchange goods or services in predetermined fashion.

applet An independent Java application, composed of self-contained code. It is usually imported into another program for a specific purpose. Applets can provide password protection, interactive forms, animation, and other programs in an HTML environment. They can also be used by programmers who have only a slight grasp of Java. See also **Java**.

autoresponder An e-mail function that automatically sends a prefabricated response to anyone who e-mails a particular address. Autoresponders are a particularly helpful way to confirm receipt of a customer concern or problem, although they are not a substitute for genuine customer service.

backbone A main line of Internet communication, composed of wires and other related mechanisms. Backbones are the physical embodiment of the so-called information superhighway.

bandwidth The carrying capacity of any Internet wire pathway. The greater the bandwidth, the more signals, or traffic, the wire can handle.

banner The most popular form of Internet advertisement. Usually rectangular in shape, banners are found in the margins of many Web pages. They are almost always clickable images, meaning that they serve as graphical links to the advertiser's own Web site.

batch transfer The movement of customer orders from the online system to a company's internal systems. Batch transfers are performed only at certain times of the day, usually either once or twice. After the batch transfer is completed, the order fulfillment process can begin.

bit The smallest unit of computer data, it can be only one of two digits: 0 or 1. (Bit is short for binary digit.) See also **bps, byte.**

bot See **spider.**

bps Bits per second. Refers to the transfer rate of information from one source to another. *Kbps*, or kilobits per second, indicates 1000 bps; *Mbps*, or megabits per second, indicates 1 million bps. See also **bit.**

bricks-and-mortar The term used to describe a traditional, real-life store, as opposed to an online company.

browser The software program that allows a person to download and display material from the Internet. It's what everybody uses to surf the Web.

button ad Essentially, a mini banner ad. Ad space for a button advertisement can usually be had for a good price, considering its small size. Still, a little ad is a lot less likely to catch the public's eye.

byte Eight bits. See also **bit.**

certificate See **digital certificate.**

charge back The refund that occurs when a customer successfully disputes an amount that was charged onto his credit card. The money is removed from the business's account and replaced in the customer's account. Charge backs are to be avoided at all costs—if a company has more than a 1 percent charge-back rate, it is in danger of having its merchant status revoked.

chat room An online location where people can communicate in real time. They can read other people's messages, post their own notes, or carry on discussions. Unlike other forms of Internet communication, chat rooms nearly always indicate the actual presence of participants.

check box A type of form in which the customer picks one or more options from a given list by clicking on the boxes next to the selections. See also **form**.

click The act of selecting an object or action on the screen.

clickable image Any graphic that performs a function when a user clicks on it. Most serve as a link to a different site; others result in some other form of action.

click-through The action that occurs when anyone uses a link to access a different Web site. Click-throughs are valued by marketing departments, who use them as a measure of customer traffic.

compatibility The quality of two different operations systems or programs being able to function with one another's code.

cookies Text files that record a person's activities while at a particular Web site; they are then are placed on a visitor's computer when she leaves the site. Cookies are stored in the COOKIES.TXT file on the surfer's terminal, although they can be erased if the user so desires. Although some people argue that they constitute an invasion of privacy, most maintain that cookies are vital for a high degree of online customer service.

CPM Cost per thousand, with the "M" representing the Roman numeral. CPM is usually used to indicate the price of an Internet advertisement. The charge is assigned on a flat fee basis for every one thousand page views the ad receives. This is also currently the most popular method of online ad payment.

crawler See **spider**.

cross-posting The act of posting identical ad material on more than one message board or newsgroup site. Cross-posting is generally frowned upon by the virtual community.

CTR Click-through rate. The percentage of customers who click through an ad every time it gets downloaded onto a screen. A normal CTR is approximately 3 percent.

cyberspace A synonym for the Internet and its environs.

cybersquatting Slang for the action taken when someone purchases a URL or domain specifically for the purpose of extorting money from anyone who wants to use it legitimately.

data mining The systematic retrieval and interpretation of previously stored information. Data mining is used to gather knowledge about people and activities, which is then used to further the efficacy of the company and to enhance the customer's experience.

dedicated access Indefinite Internet access. The user is not kicked off of the connection after a given period of activity. Both frame relay and DSL systems offer dedicated access. See also **frame relay** and **DSL**.

demand draft A substitute for check payment that does not require the paying party to be physically present at the point of purchase. Demand drafts are printed by a special company at the behest of the customer, then cashed by the merchant's bank.

destination location A Web site that people visit in order to find information. People will go online specifically to hit a destination location—it is updated on a frequent basis, thus providing surfers with a reason to return often.

dial-up See **POTS**.

digital authentication A method by which a third party confirms the identity of the recipient during an online transaction. The purpose is to safeguard the personal and financial data of the individual making the purchase. If everything checks out, the third party issues the merchant a digital certificate. See also **digital certificate**.

digital certificate A guarantee of legitimacy issued by a third party to an online merchant. The third party investigates the background of the Internet company to establish that it is not a fraudulent site; this is known as authentication. The merchant can then post the certificate on his Web site as proof of reliability. See also **digital authentication**.

discussion board A particularly structured, more formal message board that is devoted to a particular topic. While message boards are fairly open, the discussion board moderator will generally remove any off-topic content and punish any repeat abusers of the accepted ground rules.

discussion list A series of e-mails that are formatted similarly to a discussion board. Participants in the group receive a particular topic via e-mail; they can then post replies that will be sent to all other members of the group. Discussion lists are a bit more aggressive, because the e-mails are sent to the member, rather than the company needing to wait for the customer to visit the site to participate.

disintermediation The act of removing the intermediary, or middleman, from any multi-stage process. In e-commerce, it refers to the streamlining that has occurred in production since the advent of the Internet.

dithering The creation of new colors by interspersing normal pixels on the screen. Dithering is the action a monitor takes when it encounters colors with which it is unfamiliar. Usually, the effect is rather tacky. See also **pixel**.

domain name The unique set of characters—in the form of a name—given to a Web site. Domain names are used to locate a specific Internet site. See also **domain suffix**.

domain suffix Three-letter additions to a domain name that indicate a particular network. Networks are generally organized by broad topics. Currently, United States domain suffixes include the following:

.com: general businesses

.edu: educational institutions (usually colleges and universities)

.org: non-profit organizations

.net: network providers (roughly equivalent to .com)

.gov: government

Foreign domain suffixes vary by country.

download To request and receive files from another computer or system. This is the opposite of upload, which is to send files. See also **upload**.

dpi Dots per inch. Dpi is used to refer to the number of pixels within a square inch on a computer screen. The greater the dpi, the sharper the image will be.

DSL DSL is a newer form of Internet access. It provides the dedicated access of framework relay, but at lower prices. See **dedicated access, xDSL**.

e-commerce The term is applied rather loosely to include all business interactions conducted through electronic media.

ECP Excessive cross-posting. The act of cross-posting on too many different message boards or newsgroups. ECP is considered to be akin to spamming, but it has been granted its own slang name: velveeta. See also **cross-posting, velveeta**.

electronic check A check that is created and cashed online; a bank at which the customer maintains an account handles the transaction to guarantee legitimacy.

e-mail Electronic mail. Communication that is sent through a network to specific personal addresses, arriving in almost an instant.

encryption The encoding of electronic messages, used to provide security for financial or otherwise sensitive transactions. Both encryption and decryption are performed by the computer.

e-wallet The online manifestation of a real wallet. A customer places money into a special account in advance, then can spend the money like cash at participating e-tailers. E-wallets are most useful for micropayments, since there is no surcharge for their use.

Extranet similar to Intranets in that they are restricted, but they can be accessed by specific authorized individuals and organizations outside of the computer network, rather than inside. They are protected by password. See also **Intranet**.

e–zine The Internet equivalent of a magazine. Created as a special mass e-mailing, an e-zine includes articles, interviews, or other "fun" information that might be of interest to the subscriber. E-zines are subtle ads.

fail–over The term used to describe a temporary network or server failure.

FAQ Frequently Asked Questions (pronounced "fack"). FAQ lists are generated by companies in anticipation of common customer questions. The goal is to satisfy customer needs quickly while also freeing salespeople to spend their time more efficiently.

file compression The act of reducing the size of a file so that it is both less bulky and easier to download. Graphic files are virtually always compressed, although the exact protocol may differ.

firewall Often described as a technological drawbridge, firewalls are secure software intermediaries that monitor and regulate access to a company's internal files. Firewalls are built to protect companies that link their sensitive internal systems with their Web site. It's just another layer of protection.

flame An angry, insulting e-mail or post on a Web site. It is not considered acceptable to personally attack other people over the Internet or e-mail system. *Flaming* is the act of sending flames, and *flamers* are the people who create them.

form An Internet application that allows for user interaction. Forms provide some type of blank field or field for surfers to fill in. Forms are one of the most efficient ways to obtain customer feedback.

frame relay A type of Internet access usually favored by big corporations. It provides dedicated access, but at a far higher price than a standard POTS connection. It is designed for use on a network of computers. See also **POTS, dedicated access**.

FTP File Transfer Protocol. Also known as "uploading," programmers ftp material when they transfer HTML files from the personal computer to the server. Essentially, it's the act of getting large amounts of material from a disk drive to your Web site.

fulfillment The act of collecting, packing, and shipping an order. Order fulfillment is one of the best activities for a company to outsource. Turnkeys often handle such duties. See also **turnkey**.

GIF Graphical Interchange Format. The file format generally used to transfer basic graphic files on the Internet. GIF is capable of supporting a 256-color image; this is relatively basic, so GIF formatting is best used for simple graphics.

GIGO Garbage in, garbage out. This computer maxim has been around for decades, but it still applies. Anything that goes into your Web site flawed will not be magically fixed by the computer. If any changes do occur, they will likely make the original problem worse. This is especially true of scanned images. Only scan good quality pictures, or the results will be poor quality.

hacker A gifted programmer who illegally accesses sensitive information over the Internet. Some hackers are fairly harmless; they just want to nose around. Others are full-fledged criminals who perpetrate electronic fraud and engage in various degrees of theft. Hackers usually target unencrypted transmissions, which is why such stringent security measures must be taken.

hit One download of a particular Web page by a browser. Hits do *not* necessarily distinguish between visitors. They can only measure the number of times a page was requested.

homepage The main page of a Web site. Homepages usually serve as a combination introduction/table of contents.

hop One detour en route to the Internet backbone. Information has to travel through various minor paths and routers before it reaches a main line; each delay or direction change is thus referred to as a hop. The fewer hops between a user and the backbone, the better and faster the access.

host The Web site or terminal that is supporting a screen or series of actions. The host is the opposite of a user. See also **user**.

HTML HyperText Markup Language. The current standard Internet language; it is popular largely because of its simplicity. It is used mainly to format documents and import files. See also **hypertext**.

hypertext Any Internet text that contains links or other coded connections between itself and other files.

icon A small, clickable graphic that is used to represent an Internet file or function.

impression See **page impression**.

in-line ad An advertisement that runs on one side of a Web page from top to bottom; essentially, an in-line ad is a vertical banner. See also **banner**.

input box A type of form in which the customer types in his own information. There are no preselected choices or options. It's completely free-response. See also **form**.

Internet A huge network of computers that can be accessed by anyone using the correct protocols and a Web browser.

Intranet Essentially, an internal Internet. Instead of granting universal access to anyone with a browser, only authorized computers on a certain network are able to gain admittance. Intranets are usually password-protected to safeguard secure information.

IP address The Internet Protocol address. It's a series of numbers that are used by computers to locate a particular Web site on the Internet. This is not to be confused with a URL. See also **URL**.

ISDN Integrated Services Digital Network. A dial-up connection that relies on improved digital signals rather than the traditional analog type. Most small businesses are currently using ISDN, as are customers. Soon, however, ISDN will be eclipsed by DSL connections.

ISP Internet Service Provider. Companies that grant large-scale access to the Internet and charge customers for the privilege. Many ISPs will provide other services for an additional fee.

Java A popular programming language, created by Sun Microsystems. It is currently used to supplement HTML for online formatting and function. Java code allows for animation and other complex actions that are difficult to arrange with HTML. Because fewer people know Java, Sun Microsystems has begun making independent capsules available, which can be integrated with an HTML document. Such capsules are called applets. See also **applet**.

jello Internet slang for the reprehensible combination of unsolicited mass e-mails and ECP—also known as too much spam and velveeta.

JPEG Joint Photographic Experts Group. JPEG is a formatting protocol that specially compresses complex images. JPEG works especially well on photographs, although the increased detail may cause a JPEG file to load more slowly than the simpler GIF graphic.

key A code that is used to encrypt and decrypt encoded electronic messages. When a secure transmission is sent from one computer to another, only the two computers involved will have the proper key; this helps prevent transmissions from being intercepted by hackers.

link An address embedded in a Web document. When visitors click on the link, they are automatically taken to the pertinent location. Links can either be internal, meaning they lead to a different page within the site, or they can be external, which entails a trip to an entirely different URL.

list box A type of form in which the user selects only one choice from a preselected drop-down list of options. See also **form**.

mailing list When used properly, it's a group of opt-in e-mail addresses that are used as a directory for mass e-mailings. If the mail is unsolicited, then the mailing list becomes a spamming device. See also **spam**.

mass customization The large-scale production of adaptive material. Mass customization allows a big corporation to respond individually to each visitor's needs, even if the number of customers is in the thousands. Such flexibility is written into the site, through the use of interactivity and target marketing.

message board An Internet location where participants can post messages on a variety of topics, then receive feedback from other visitors. Message boards are different from chat rooms in that they are more structured and do not take place in real time.

meta tags The formatting codes specially placed near the top of an HTML document to convey descriptive information to passing search engine spiders. They are not visible on a normal page view, but the spiders scan code and pick up the information. The data gleaned from meta tags is used to help categorize the Web site for placement in search engine listings. See also **search engine, spider**.

micropayment Payments that are too small to be effectively paid for on an individual basis. They are held in a special account until a prearranged figure is reached, then the appropriate credit card is charged.

MID Merchant Identification Number. An MID is used by the acquirer to positively identify each merchant in a transaction.

modem A tool that allows data to pass back and forth from computer screen to telephone line. It's basically a complex translator.

moderator A neutral individual who prompts Internet discussion forums and message boards, then monitors subsequent exchanges between participants. As a behavioral control, the moderator has the power to both grant and deny access to the discussion. See also **discussion board**.

NAP Network Access Point. The spot at which data can merge with an Internet backbone. See also **backbone**.

network A group of linked computers that can share information; these computers may or may not be in geographic proximity.

newbie An Internet novice, or a person who is new to a particular Web site.

newsgroup Sort of a formal discussion group, in which one topic is posed by a moderator and any interested individual can post topical comments or questions. See also **discussion list.**

niche A small corner of the general consumer market; it is usually focused on one particular interest or trait.

object-oriented programming A form of programming that focuses on content and compatibility, so that the resulting applications can work with various other programs without needing to be adjusted. The details are not important for a manager to know, but be aware that Java is a good example.

online To be connected to the Internet.

online purchasing The area of a Web site that allows for actual online transactions. Customers enter the pertinent data, place an order, and money changes hands (albeit electronically). Online purchasing sites do not yet show up in many virtual stores, but the percentage is rapidly growing. See also **online shopping.**

online shopping The area of a Web site that helps lead the customer towards a purchasing decision. It plays a crucial supportive role by answering customer questions, providing information about the company, offering product information, and much more. In fact, online shopping encompasses everything on a Web site except for the actual purchase process itself. See also **online purchasing.**

outsourcing The hiring of an outside company to accomplish specific tasks for the paying business. Outsourcing is particularly helpful to companies that have a minimum of resources.

page impression In all important respects, a page impression is the same thing as a page view—simply one request from a computer to download the files for one Web page.

PC A personal computer. Basically, it's what you have on your desk at home or work.

pixel Short for "picture element." A pixel is the smallest element of color or light on a monitor. The more pixels there are in a given area, the more complex and sharp the screen images will be.

plug-in The little extras that can be downloaded onto your browser for increased performance or new capabilities. Programs that play streaming video, high-quality sound, or other multimedia files are all examples of plug-ins. Although they are often free, most surfers do not make use of them.

pop-ups Pop-up windows are advertisements that load in advance of the Web page to which they are linked. They appear as a page is downloading, and are superimposed on the page proper. Most customers find them highly annoying, but they can be undeniably effective.

portal Any major destination site on the Internet, where some people arrive online immediately dialing up. Search engines are excellent examples of portals.

post As a noun, it means a public message or file placed onto a Web page. As a verb it means to actually place an online post.

POTS Plain old telephone service. The traditional small business and consumer mode of Internet access. It requires a dial-up connection, which means that the signals are sent out straight over the telephone line. Due to limits on capacity, subscribers with POTS are kicked offline if they spend more than a few minutes inactively. Still the prices are fairly low.

protocol A set of data standards that programmers agree on to enable efficient communication between computers on a network.

Public Key Infrastructure Provides public, guaranteed electronic security keys to companies and individuals. As a third party, the PKI is usually above reproach, which helps enhance the safety of the transmission.

radio button A type of form in which the customer can choose only one option from a small set of choices. Radio buttons are circular, and only one can be selected at a time. See also **form**.

real-time An action that takes place on screen, with no time delay.

resolution The sharpness or clarity of a graphic image. Dpi is often used to describe resolution in exact terms. See also **dpi**.

robot See **spider**.

router A computer that is used to link communication between two networks. Individual routers are often referred to as a hop when data is making its way towards the backbone. See also **hop, backbone**.

scanner A device that reads and translates hard copy documents into electronic, Internet-compatible files. If a user desires to post new images or photos onto a Web site, a scanner is an absolute necessity. *Scanning* is the act of using a scanner.

scrolling The act of adjusting a single Web page that cannot fit entirely on the computer screen at one time. Scrolling is used to bring different areas of the page into view.

search directory A Web service that maintains a database of all URLs that have visited the directory and requested inclusion. Customers can enter a phrase or keyword, thus requesting any addresses that relate to the given information. The results are then categorized according to self-reported description and posted. Directories are not to be confused with search engines, although they are often referred to as such in a general context.

search engine A Web service that maintains a database of all URLs that it has discovered through the use of spiders, which is a *lot*. Customers can enter a phrase or keyword, thus requesting any addresses that relate to the given information. The results are categorized in a manner unique to the particular engine, then posted. See also **spider**.

secure server A server that ensures that all data entered on a Web site is encrypted and sent along protected channels. See also **server**.

server A computer that serves as the focal point for a network. It manages communications and applications for all involved terminals.

shopping cart An icon that is used on most Web sites that support online purchasing. It permits a shopper to save selections made during the current visit, so that they can be purchased all at once.

S–HTTP Secure HyperText Transfer Protocol. S-HTTP is just one more type of secure protocol used to encrypt and host sensitive transmissions.

site ranking The numerical placement of a Web site on a search engine listing. Although a company's ranking varies according to search engine, and is rarely the same number twice even at the same engine, there is still a basic principle to work towards: You want as high a ranking as possible— this means trying to get a low number, as in golf! Site ranking can be improved in a number of ways, largely by altering the content posted at the top of the homepage. The more focused the site is on a particular topic, the better its ranking will be.

snail mail The slightly condescending computer term for regular old stationery- and-stamps mail. In other words, it's the slower alternative to e-mail.

spam Unsolicited mass e-mail, almost always in the form of advertisements or other marketing material. Most Internet surfers hate spam with a passion, largely because they see it as an invasion of personal space.

spider An automated program that is designed by programmers of search engines to comb the Internet looking for new Web sites. Alternatively referred to as "robots," "bots," or "crawlers," spiders scan a Web site for information in particular locations, then transmit the data back to the search engine. Spiders also read and process meta tags. See **meta tags**.

splash page An optional addition to a Web site, a splash page is a prehomepage introduction. It might carry a couple graphics, along with the company logo and a brief description of the site. Splash pages always lead directly (and solely) to the site homepage.

spoofing The imitation of an established Web site on the Internet. Spoofing is mostly accomplished by obtaining a URL that is nearly identical to the victim's. Sometimes it is harmless, done either for comic effect or to grab attention. Usually, however, it's an earmark of fraud. When done for a criminal purpose, the spoofers imitate the victim site as closely as possible, then try to obtain the credit card information of the unsuspecting "customer."

SSL Secure Socket Layer. SSL is a particular type of encryption that is used to protect secure transmissions over the Internet.

start-up The term used to describe an online company that originated in cyberspace, as opposed to a bricks-and-mortar company that moved online. See also **bricks-and-mortar**.

streaming The continual transfer of information from server to network computer; it usually refers to sound or video files. They look or sound smoother when used in this format.

surf To travel around on the Internet, not necessarily with a purpose. A *surfer* is someone who surfs.

tags See **meta tags**.

template A software package that is preformed to accept data in a certain format. Templates help novices design successful applications without being experts on the programming language or other material.

TIN Terminal Identification Number. Yet another serial number used by an acquirer to distinguish between individual merchants. This number is permanent as long as the merchant maintains a business relationship with the acquirer.

traffic The number of people who visit a particular Web site or page.

turnkey A company that receives and performs certain types of outsource work for various businesses. Typically, turnkeys have handled order processing and fulfillment, but now they are branching out onto the Internet as well, offering more comprehensive services.

unique A term used to describe a person as being distinct from other visitors and from that same person's previous visit. Uniqueness is what counts when marketing executives must analyze data that includes page views and hits. See also **page impression, hit**.

upload The act of sending a file to another computer. This is the opposite of the more commonly referenced *download,* which is to receive a file. See also **download**.

URL Uniform Resource Locator. Unlike a simple domain name, the URL is the whole Internet address: http//:www.yadayada.com.

user Any individual who utilizes an Internet program or service. Users are on the receiving end of the interaction.

velveeta Internet slang for ECP. See also **cross-posting, ECP**.

virtual Anything that is described as virtual pertains to cyberspace or the Internet. It's used in the sense of "almost," since cyberspace is "almost" real.

virtual mall A grouping of unrelated stores on the Internet, similar in form to real-life malls. Although the initial virtual mall concept was not a success, online turnkeys are beginning to use such groupings as a way of collectively handling their clients. Malls do not generally have a big effect; most consumers are not even aware of the structure when they visit each individual store.

virus A pernicious computer program that invades and destroys both networks and individual computers. Viruses are generally spread through e-mail, in the form of attachments that are appended to a host message. The attachment must be physically opened by the recipient in order to cause any harm; most experts thus recommend the deletion of all e-mail from strangers that includes attachments.

Webmaster A common title for the person who maintains and improves a Web site, nearly always tinkering with the site on a full-time basis. If a company can possibly handle the expense, it should definitely hire at least one employee who can focus solely on the virtual store; this would be the Webmaster.

Web page A group of text and/or graphic files that can be viewed with a browser.

Web site Related Web pages that are linked together, virtually always belonging to the same individual or institution. See also **Web page**.

World Wide Web The common representation of the Internet, complete with graphic Web sites and all other necessary elements. In other words, it's the Internet's user interface.

xDSL Standard shorthand for an inclusive reference to DSL technology; it encompasses all variations of the standard DSL line. The "x" stands in place of where the extra, identifying letter is located for each type of DSL. See also **DSL**.

XML eXtensible Markup Language. This is the latest alternative to HTML, and is being hailed as a great improvement. While it can support traditional HTML files, it has greater flexibility than the older language and better compatibility with other programming languages. It focuses on content rather than format, which aids in the transfer of information.

zine See **e-zine.**

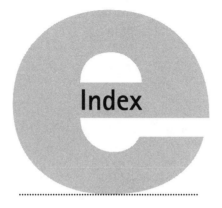

Index